Second Edition

溝通 # Making Connections

Enhance Your Listening Comprehension in Chinese

Traditional Character Version

Madeline K. Spring

CHENG & TSUI COMPANY

Boston

Published by
Cheng & Tsui Company, Inc.
25 West Street
Boston, MA 02111-1213 USA
Fax (617) 426-3669
www.cheng-tsui.com
"Bringing Asia to the World"™

Traditional Character Version
ISBN 978-0-88727-665-1

Simplified Character Version
ISBN 978-0-88727-767-2

Printed in the United States of America

Audio Downloads

Users of this book have free access to downloadable audio recordings. To download them, you simply need to register your product key on Cheng & Tsui's website.

Instructions:

1. Visit the Cheng & Tsui download center at www.cheng-tsui.com/downloads and follow the instructions for creating a user account.

2. Register your product key.

3. Download the files.

For technical support, please contact support@cheng-tsui.com or call 1-800-554-1963.

Your Product Key: URAB-YPU7

Titles of Related Interest

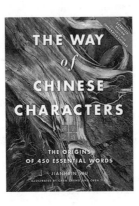

Integrated Chinese, Third Edition
By Yuehua Liu, Tao-chung Yao, et al.

The leading introductory Chinese textbook series at colleges, universities, and high schools around the world.

The Way of Chinese Characters
The Origins of 450 Essential Words
By Jianhsin Wu, Illustrated by Chen Zheng, Chen Tian

An illustrated guide to the history behind the vocabulary in *Integrated Chinese* Level 1 Part 1.

Tales and Traditions
Readings in Chinese Literature Series
Compiled by Yun Xiao, et al.

Level-appropriate adaptations of Chinese legends and folktales.

Visit **www.cheng-tsui.com** to view samples, place orders, and browse other language-learning materials.

CONTENTS 目錄

Acknowledgments

Many people have been involved with various aspects of this project—no one could have imagined its complexity when we began our work a number of years ago.

I deeply appreciate the contributions of the speakers whose voices form the texts for the lessons. Recording "spontaneous" conversations in the cramped confines of a sound studio and making them sound authentic is truly an art, and I have been fortunate to work with such talented people, who accomplished this so gracefully. Most of these men and women were graduate students at the University of Colorado, Boulder. They include Wang Wei, Wang Ping, Shelley Wing Chan, Haning Hughes, Liu Yingnan, Zhang Dongming, Zhang Huicong, Wang Yanning, Wang Fengtao, Lu Xiaoyin, Rebecca Li, Liu Changli, and Zhang Huijie. Special thanks also to Shelley Wing Chan, Howard Y.F. Choy, Kong Mei, and Shen Ning for their valuable input at various stages of the project that resulted in the first edition of *Making Connections.* Similarly, Sandy Adler, Richard Borkowski, Brett Mann, and Dave Underwood were all instrumental in helping format the text, producing the audio recordings, and designing the original book cover for that edition.

Production of the second edition of *Making Connections* has involved several talented people at Arizona State University. I am especially grateful to Ryan Robbins for his innovative artwork and creative graphics and painstaking efforts updating the text. I would also like to acknowledge Jie Zhu and Jing Xia for their help translating the new introduction into Chinese. Jie Zhu also deserves considerable thanks for her helpful suggestions about ways to make the introduction more useful to teachers of Chinese. Both Minying Tan and Sam Lasser at Cheng & Tsui worked patiently to improve and update *Making Connections.* Errors in the first edition have been corrected, and having the audio files online in MP3 form will make the sound segments easily accessible to students.

But mostly I would like to thank Jill Cheng for her ongoing support of this project. A pioneer in the field of publication of Chinese materials, Jill is a longtime champion of innovation in the field of Teaching Chinese as a Foreign Language. Her willingness to publish a textbook that is completely focused on unscripted, naturally-paced Chinese reflects her vision and commitment to providing a variety of resources that facilitate successful language learning and high levels of cultural competence.

I believe this book will help fill a gap in instructional resources for Chinese as teachers and students can use it in the manner that best suits their needs. I am eager to hear feedback about their experiences and about ways the book can be improved.

Introduction

To the Teacher

Without altering the spirit of *Making Connections*, we have implemented significant changes in the second edition. Primarily we have updated the look and feel of the visuals throughout the book, so that it is more inviting to today's students.

This text offers an exciting way for learners of Mandarin to develop and improve their aural comprehension skills. The need for an innovative textbook in Chinese that focuses primarily on listening comprehension, and that is flexible enough so it can be implemented directly into various curricula, is keen. The conversations in this textbook are presented in authentic and naturally paced language, and the lessons are constructed to support students' existing knowledge and develop mastery of new and recycled vocabulary, grammatical structures, and sociocultural practices.

The main objective of *Making Connections* is to equip students with listening strategies that will improve their comprehension of naturally spoken Chinese. Higher levels of proficiency in listening readily transfer to other language skills. Students who use *Making Connections* show demonstrable gains in their ability to understand spoken Chinese, which in turn has a dynamic impact on their overall ability to communicate effectively in Chinese.

Target Learners

Making Connections is designed for students who have **completed at least one semester of college-level Mandarin or one year of an introductory-level high school program.** It can be used effectively as a supplementary text in a second-semester first-year college course, or in a second- or third-year college course. Students in AP or IB high school classes also enjoy the challenge of working with the authentic, naturally-paced conversations in each lesson. *Making Connections* appeals to students of all ages and backgrounds who want to work independently on reviewing or improving their listening comprehension. Even advanced students and heritage Chinese learners who are already familiar with the vocabulary used in the conversations in this text are surprised by how much they learn from working with audio texts that model the ways idiomatic expressions and other vocabulary items are actually used.

Focus on Strategic Listening

Listening comprehension is often overlooked in Chinese courses. Nonetheless, most teachers agree that students need significant access to multiple forms of comprehensible input in order to function successfully in Chinese-speaking situations. *Making Connections* provides this input in a conversational format that engages students' interest.

Before students can use new vocabulary and grammatical patterns in meaningful ways, they need to be exposed to natural speech that occurs in normal conversation. When comprehension skills are presented systematically, students are better equipped to cope with linguistic situations that may be slightly beyond their level. As confidence in dealing with these situations builds, students are willing to take greater risks in producing their own language, and their attitudes toward learning the language become even more positive. The strategies learned in improving listening comprehension undoubtedly help students improve in reading comprehension and other aspects of language learning.

Each lesson guides students from getting the gist of the audio text to listening for specific details. The section "Key Language Points" focuses on particular idiomatic usages or grammatical structures that frequently confuse language learners. Although students have encountered many of these phrases previously, they may not yet have the confidence to incorporate them into their own language production. Drawing attention to specific usage helps students notice these expressions and hear how they are used contextually. As research in Second Language Acquisition has proven, explicit awareness of language usage or "noticing" is an integral part of the language learning process. By incorporating *Making Connections* into their curriculum, teachers can direct students' attention to how particular aspects of the spoken language function in actual discourse. Students become familiar with hearing language functions such as paraphrasing, asking for clarification, expressing agreement or disagreement, inferring, elaborating, hesitating, and repeating. These aspects of oral discourse differ from written texts, which is what learners generally study, since oral speech happens spontaneously and is unplanned.

Descriptions of Proficiency Levels

The ACTFL Guidelines offer a rough standard to describe listening abilities at various stages in the learner's proficiency development. Teachers and students should keep these guidelines in mind when using *Making Connections*. Below is a handy chart that describes the kinds of listening tasks students are able to perform at different levels of proficiency.[1]

ACTFL Proficiency Level	Descriptions
Novice-Mid	Able to understand some short, learned utterances, particularly where context strongly supports understanding and speech is clearly audible. Comprehends some words and phrases from simple questions, statements, high-frequency commands and courtesy formulae about topics that refer to basic personal information or the immediate physical setting. The listener requires long pauses for assimilation and periodically requests repetition and/or a slower rate of speech.
Novice-High	Able to understand short, learned utterances and some sentence-length utterances, particularly where context strongly supports understanding and speech is clearly audible. Comprehends words and phrases from simple questions, statements, high-frequency commands, and courtesy formulae. May require repetition, rephrasing, and/or a slowed rate of speech for comprehension.
Intermediate-Low	Able to understand sentence-length utterances, which consist of recombination of learned elements in a limited number of content areas, particularly if strongly supported by the situational context. Content refers to basic personal background and needs, social conventions and routine tasks, such as getting meals and receiving simple instructions and directions. Listening tasks pertain primarily to spontaneous face-to-face conversations. Understanding is often uneven; repetition and rewording may be necessary. Misunderstandings in both main ideas and details arise frequently.

[1] Retrieved from http://www.sil.org/lingualinks/languagelearning/otherresources/actflproficiencyguidelines/ACTFLGuidelines ListeningInterm.htm.

ACTFL Proficiency Level	Descriptions
Intermediate-Mid	Able to understand sentence-length utterances, which consist of recombination of learned utterances on a variety of topics. Content continues to refer primarily to basic personal background and needs, social conventions and somewhat more complex tasks, such as lodging, transportation, and shopping. Additional content areas include some personal interests and activities, and a greater diversity of instructions and directions. Listening tasks not only pertain to spontaneous face-to-face conversations but also to short routine telephone conversations and some deliberate speech, such as simple announcements and reports over the media. Understanding continues to be uneven.
Intermediate High	Able to sustain understanding over longer stretches of connected discourse on a number of topics pertaining to different times and places; however, understanding is inconsistent due to failure to grasp main ideas and/or details. Thus, while topics do not differ significantly from those of an Advanced level listener, comprehension is less in quantity and poorer in quality.
Advanced	Able to understand main ideas and most details of connected discourse on a variety of topics beyond the immediacy of the situation. Comprehension may be uneven due to a variety of linguistic and extra linguistic factors, among which topic familiarity is very prominent. These texts frequently involve description and narration in different time frames or aspects, such as present, no past, habitual, or imperfective. Texts may include interviews, short lectures on familiar topics, and news items and reports primarily dealing with factual information. Listener is aware of cohesive devices but may not be able to use them to follow the sequence of thought in an oral text.

Setting Realistic Expectations

Improving listening comprehension is a process. As such, *Making Connections* helps teachers and students set realistic expectations about how to get the most out of listening to native speech, rather than expecting 100% comprehension of each utterance.

Instructors need not worry that students cannot grasp every word of the conversations or that some of the language used is too colloquial or too challenging. Teachers should also avoid the temptation to transcribe the dialogues for students. Giving students a script of what is said in the dialogue defeats the purpose of guiding students toward comprehension of natural speech. Keep in mind that the teaching objective is for students to improve their listening skills so they can catch what is being said at a normal pace by speakers who are not making accommodations for the linguistic level of their audience.

Your students' ability to work with the audio segments in *Making Connections* may surprise you. Remember that they pick up a lot from contextual clues and they also gain familiarity with the voices they hear. Don't worry if they think the speakers talk too fast. As their listening skills improve, they will soon imagine that these same speakers have actually slowed down!

The use of realia in *Making Connections* (newspaper advertisements, receipts, medical prescriptions, etc.) exposes students to authentic Chinese writing at early stages of their language acquisition process. The tasks that involve these authentic texts are generally quite simple—in fact, the most important part of these exercises is for students to see what "real Chinese" looks like. This aspect of *Making Connections* promotes cultural awareness, which is one of the important pedagogical standards for effective foreign language learning.

Integrating *Making Connections* into Your Curriculum

Making Connections is not intended to function as a main textbook. Grammar explanations are given sparingly, and there is little emphasis on reading. It is assumed that students will gain adequate exposure to work in these areas through their primary textbooks. A minimum of preparation is required for the instructor, and the lessons can easily be assigned to complement regular course materials. Although it is tempting to simply correlate topics between *Making Connections* and the regular first-year textbook, this approach is often not the best pedagogically. Rather, teachers should first consider the language level of the students and make sure it matches that in the audio files. Students enjoy following the sequential interactions between the main speakers in Part I (Lessons 1–23); this aspect of the text will be diminished if the lessons are taught in a random order.

The order and topics of the lessons in Part I are generally coordinated with *Integrated Chinese* Level 1, with some discrepancies in topics between *Making Connections*, Second Edition and *Integrated Chinese*, Third Edition. However, these lessons should **not** be used at the same time that these topics are first introduced. The goal is to review and recycle material that is familiar to students. While *Making Connections* is an ideal accompaniment to *Integrated Chinese*, it does not need to be used in that way. It can certainly stand alone as a listening comprehension component of courses that use other texts, or as a product for self-learners or heritage students who already have some background in Mandarin.

Most of the lessons in *Making Connections* are targeted to learners who are at the Novice-Mid/High level. By this time, learners have already had exposure to many of the topics and are ready to hear conversations that recycle language they studied previously. At the same time, the introduction of limited new material does not interfere with their linguistic progress.

Remember that working with listening comprehension need not take much classroom time; most of the work can be done as homework or posted online.

Applying Best Practices in Recycling and Spiraling

Language learning does not take place in a linear manner. Students need frequent practice and review of previously learned material. Current textbooks address this issue to some extent, but nonetheless constant repetition of the same type of textbook material can sometimes be boring and frustrating for students. This is especially true for students in the Novice-High to Intermediate-Low levels.

Two principles of Second Language Acquisition are key to using this material:

- Vocabulary needs constant and **consistent review and recycling** in order to become fixed in the learner's long-term memory.
- Exposure to vocabulary and points of language usage must occur in **multiple contexts.**

Frequently, teachers are so focused on preparing and presenting new material that they neglect these two important pedagogical principles. *Making Connections* offers a systematic way to recycle and spiral previously-studied topics using naturally-paced materials that draw students' attention to specific listening strategies and toward improving listening comprehension. Through controlled practice on familiar topics, students interact with vocabulary and points of language usage in different contexts, presented in interactive and engaging formats. A minimum of new material is incorporated in each lesson; the main teaching objective is for students to gain control of a few key points that are emphasized explicitly. This allows students to study new material presented in their main textbook, while they enjoy a slightly freer and more expansive learning experience with *Making Connections*. Students have multiple chances to gain confidence with both previously-studied and new materials, allowing them to move readily from conceptual control to partial control and eventually to full control, as is illustrated below:

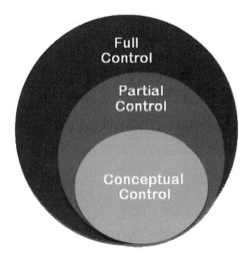

Improving Curricular Articulation

Teachers frequently have students with a variety of skills and backgrounds in the same class. Supplementary, controlled practice in recycling and spiraling vocabulary, structures, and language functions helps individuate learning since students themselves determine how many times they listen to each audio file. *Making Connections* can be a useful resource to bridge gaps between the core curricular texts used in different levels of Chinese. This is essential, since often students have gaps in their learning (summer, winter breaks, etc.) and need options for catching up or moving ahead toward higher levels of language proficiency. As students progress from beginning to intermediate to advanced to superior levels of language proficiency, they need articulated Chinese language programs to guide them. Relying entirely on one particular textbook or set of textbook materials may prove insufficient for students to achieve the measurable outcomes that objectively verify proficiency levels.

Increasing Student Motivation

Not all students learn at the same pace. Students at the Novice-Mid to Intermediate-Mid levels especially need enhanced input to improve their listening comprehension. *Making Connections* offers a common ground to all students, which lowers affective fears and creates a positive and motivating learning environment.

Working with "real" Chinese, rather than relying solely on text-based materials, is intrinsically dynamic and appealing to students. Although the language and delivery may be challenging, *Making Connections* shows students what genuine conversations between native speakers of Mandarin sound like (complete with mumbling!). Since every lesson is structured to facilitate comprehension progressively, students gain confidence in their ability to understand more of what they hear each time they listen. This sense of achievement and accomplishment is a tremendous motivating factor, which naturally leads to increases in proficiency and communicative competence.

Tolerating Language Variation

As with any language, Chinese teachers and learners need to be tolerant of times when the speakers in these conversations or monologues make grammatical or pronunciation "mistakes" or say things in ways that are different from textbook Chinese or from how the teacher speaks. Even though each of the speakers is a native speaker of Mandarin, inevitably s/he will say things in ways that are not perfectly "correct." As teachers, we need not fear that this will have a negative impact on our students—it is simply a fact that language usage varies widely. Students should understand this metalinguistic reality early on in their language learning experience. Given the dramatic impact of media and the Internet, the ease of international travel, and the extent of options for study abroad, it is increasingly difficult to categorize specific usage as belonging only to any one region. When obvious distinctions in language usage or pronunciation variance do occur in the audio selections, notes have been added. Indications of whether the term is generally associated with speakers from the PRC or Taiwan offer instructors an opportunity to point out such differences whenever relevant to curriculum or approach. Similarly, photos and realia from both the PRC and Taiwan allow students to see variety in Mandarin-speaking environments. In these ways, *Making Connections* helps bridge the gap students will encounter as they make the transition from the classroom environment to more realistic situations.

Organization and Structure of Each Lesson

The pedagogical model in *Making Connections* is founded in schema theory. Each lesson guides students through five stages, beginning with a contextualized pre-listening activity and ending with a productive language activity that allows students to express themselves both orally and in writing using vocabulary and structures they heard in the conversation or monologue.

Stage I. Preparation　熱身

Before listening to the audio segment, students need to be engaged in the topic. Stage I generally has two parts. Part 1 offers useful vocabulary that relates to what is said in the conversation or monologue. Whenever possible, visual cues help introduce vocabulary—students are asked to match the Chinese characters (sometime accompanied by *pinyin*) to the appropriate picture. Students are presented with additional limited vocabulary through short definitions in either English or Chinese, depending on the level of the lesson. Idiomatic expressions with sample sentences showing usage are also given.

Research has shown that listening comprehension improves significantly when learners are successful at activating their prior knowledge (*schemata*). Part 2 contains pre-listening activities that provide the context for the audio selection by using advance organizers to activate students' background knowledge. Brief exercises personalize and contextualize the vocabulary and concepts introduced in the dialogue and prepare students for active listening. Generally a "notepad" is provided for students to jot down notes or respond to questions in English (if students want to add *pinyin* or Chinese, they are free to do so—this is entirely for their own use and should not be collected or graded by the instructor). Another effective option is to use an online brainstorming source such as Bubbl.us (https://bubbl.us/).

Stage II. Listening for the Gist　泛聽

Now students hear the conversation for the first time. They should read these exercises first so they know what to listen for. In Stage II, students are led to discover the general points of the conversation, such as the relationship between the speakers, the location where the conversation occurs, and the main topic of conversation. These initial tasks are minimal and simple; the emphasis is on global comprehension. If students have difficulty with this section, they should listen to the segment again. Ideally, Stage II is done in a classroom setting.

Stage III. Listening for Details　靜聽

Specific, task-based exercises that require greater comprehension are introduced in Stage III. The exercises focus on what the speakers said and how they said it. Tasks include completion of tables and charts, multiple choice, true/false, matching, and cloze exercises. Depending on the level of difficulty, the exercises are either entirely in English or in a combination of English and simple Chinese. Stage III should be done beyond the classroom environment so that students can listen to the audio selection as often as desired.

Stage IV. Working with the Language　語言點

Once students have a good idea of what the speaker or speakers said, they are ready to focus on specific points of vocabulary usage, language functions, and grammatical structures. Stage IV offers a range of exercises, such as matching, sentence and dialogue completion, cloze exercises, translation, and multiple choice. Not every grammatical point or idiomatic usage that occurs in the audio segment is addressed. Instead, the goal is to highlight a few very important linguistic features. Often, these are items that students have learned previously; here they are recycled in a different context. Stage IV should be done beyond the classroom environment so that students can listen to the sound file as often as desired.

Stage V. Follow-up Activities　應用

Section V gives students a chance to practice expressing themselves in spoken and written Chinese. Each lesson offers guided activities contextually related to the conversation. Tasks include role playing, dialogue completion, writing activities (in Chinese), etc. The exercises are designed both for classroom settings and for independent work, and they are flexible enough so instructors and students can adapt them to their needs. Written assignments or oral activities can easily be uploaded to a website so students can share their work with others. Extending the audience beyond the conventional student-to-teacher focus has a dynamic impact on language production and motivation.

Contents of This Textbook

Each lesson presents a short conversation or monologue that reflects unrehearsed, native Mandarin. The speakers were not given scripts, nor was the conversation limited to specific vocabulary. In other words, this is simulated authentic language. Each lesson is accompanied by written exercises. A rough distribution of the levels is shown on the next page:

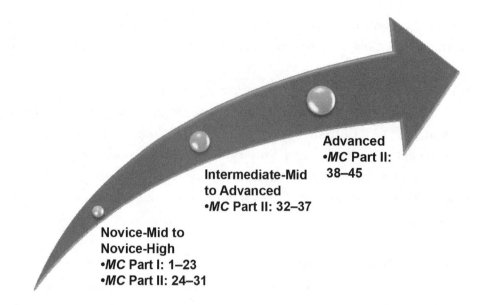

Advanced
•*MC* Part II: 38–45

Intermediate-Mid to Advanced
•*MC* Part II: 32–37

Novice-Mid to Novice-High
•*MC* Part I: 1–23
•*MC* Part II: 24–31

Instructors should note that although the language in some of the segments in Lessons 32–45 may at first seem too complex for your students, the exercises given in the lessons will help them negotiate and apply listening comprehension strategies they learned in Lessons 1–23 and 24–31 to these more complex conversations. Keep in mind that there is no expectation for them to grasp every word or nuance. The exercises for these lessons are intentionally challenging and incorporate words and phrases that may or may not have been previously introduced. This approach gives students a chance to move beyond their current level of mastery to figure out what the speakers are saying, based on context and other hints given in the exercises. This is dramatically different from what most students have encountered so far in their study of Chinese, since most conventional textbooks only include words or structures that students have formally learned and that are accepted as model examples of standard Mandarin. Students may think their progress is slow, and the exercises might seem daunting at first, but soon they will discover how much better-prepared they are to encounter situations in which authentic Chinese is spoken. For this reason, Part II (Lessons 24–45) is particularly useful and motivating for students who are preparing to go abroad or to continue with more advanced-level Chinese courses.

Part I (Lessons 1–23)

The order and topics of these lessons are generally coordinated with the lessons in *Integrated Chinese* Level 1, with some discrepancies in topics between *Making Connections*, Second Edition and *Integrated Chinese*, Third Edition. Whereas *Making Connections* is an ideal accompaniment to that text, it does not need to be used in that way. It can certainly stand alone as a listening comprehension component of courses that use other texts, or as a product for self-learners or heritage students who already have some background in Mandarin.

Part II (Lessons 24–45)

Students who have completed most of Part I and are familiar with the format and expectations of the lessons are well-prepared to engage with Lessons 24–45, which are appropriate for students at a range of listening proficiencies. Whereas the lessons in Part I present conversations between the same two speakers, Part II offers students a chance to hear a variety of speakers talking about a wide range of subjects. For the most part, these conversations or monologues are set in the United States; six lessons (Lessons 24–28 and 31) are set in China. Three lessons (Lessons 40, 41, and 45) are Chinese-language radio broadcasts that probably would be heard outside of China or Taiwan. Like Lessons 1–23, all the audio segments for Lessons 24–45 are naturally paced and unscripted.

The last eight lessons offer a challenge and a resource for guiding students toward superior-level proficiency. Several of the speakers in these later lessons have slight regional accents, and their language usage is not always grammatically perfect. These lessons provide students with a chance to practice listening to slightly non-standard Chinese, since inevitably they will have to face this situation. Instructors are urged to be tolerant with these materials and to avoid the tendency to focus on what the speakers should have said. Rather, if students follow what is emphasized in the lesson, they will profit greatly from exposure to this type of Chinese.

In response to requests from instructors and students who prefer to work more in the target language, some of the more advanced lessons include Chinese in the exercises.

* * *

Suggestions for Use in Curriculum
Model 1 — To be used with *Integrated Chinese* or another beginning/intermediate-level text

For students who have completed one semester of college-level Chinese: Part I One lesson per week (e.g., in conjunction with *Integrated Chinese* Level 1 Part 2). For students who have completed one academic year of college-level Chinese: Part I 1–3 lessons per week at the beginning of the academic session (e.g., in conjunction with *Integrated Chinese* Level 2).

In class: Last 10 minutes of class period
The instructor works with students to complete pre-listening activities. This brainstorming session can be held in Chinese or English, depending on the students' levels. The students are encouraged to work in groups or pairs. Students are introduced to the vocabulary items in Stage I of each lesson. After students have completed this stage, they read the "Listening for the Gist" exercises. Then the instructor plays the audio segments once or twice, without stopping, and allows a few minutes for students to complete the exercises (or answer the questions).

Homework assignment
Students complete Stages III and IV and submit these to the instructor for correction.

In class: Follow-up (half class period)
This session could occur later in the week, ideally after student papers have been returned. The oral activities in Stage V are particularly well-suited to classroom settings. Additional practice with vocabulary/grammar may be included as the instructor wishes. The writing and speaking activities in Stage V are best assigned as homework. These may be uploaded to a course web site and shared among peers and teachers.

Model 2 — For students who have completed two academic years of college-level Chinese

Use Part I (Lessons 1–23) intensively at the beginning of the academic year. Students should be able to work largely on their own. The written exercises can be turned in on a weekly basis or collected in a portfolio.

The lessons in Part II (Lessons 24–45) can be assigned similarly (either one lesson per week or one lesson per two weeks) for the remainder of the year. Ideally, the instructor should follow the same general model that is outlined above (i.e., working with pre-listening activities before working with the conversations themselves). In this way, teachers and students will be reminded of how integral the listening component is to their entire Chinese language curriculum. Instructors will need to decide how many of the lessons in Part II are appropriate for their students. Most students should be ready to proceed to the next group of lessons (24–31). Some instructors may want to save the more advanced segments (lessons 32–45) for work in third- or fourth-year courses, or for independent work by students who want a greater challenge.

Madeline K. Spring
January 2012

序言

致教師

《溝通：提升你的中文聽力》第二版秉承了第一版的教學理念，同時又在內容、插圖、版式上做了大量修訂更新，以期對當今學生更具吸引力。

本書主要用于訓練和提高中文學習者的聽力水平。當今中文教學亟需一本新穎、靈活的聽力教材，以配合不同的教學課程設置。本書所有對話均是自然場景下的真實對話。通過對這些真實語料的合理設置，本書有利于學習者復習、鞏固和拓展現有知識，提高中文運用能力，并加深對中文社會文化的認知。

本書主要目標在于培養學生聽力策略，提高學生聽懂自然中文對話的能力。聽力的提高有利于其他方面語言能力的進步。通過使用本書，學生不僅聽力將得到大幅強化，綜合漢語水平也將呈現顯著進步。

本書適用對象

本書的主要針對的是已學習至少一學期大學中文課程的大學生，或至少已學習一學年基礎中文課程的高中生。本書可以作為輔助教材用于大學一年級第二個學期，大學二年級，或大學三年級的中文課堂。同時，高中AP或IB中文班的學生也將會覺得本書聽力材料的真實語境、自然語速對他們既實用，又有一定的挑戰性；而具有一定基礎，正在自學中文的學習者，將會通過本書進一步鞏固和提高現有聽力水平；即使漢語程度較高的學習者或華裔學生，也將從本書丰富地道的語言材料中獲益匪淺。

聚焦策略聽力

盡管聽力訓練在漢語教學中常被忽視，但大多數教師都認為，學生必須能聽懂不同場合下的語言使用，才能在真實的漢語環境中正常交流。《溝通》正是一本把這些把不同的語言材料，用學生感興趣的對話形式呈現出來的聽力教材。

在學生能使用新詞匯、新句型做有實質意義的交流之前，他們需要首先适應自然對話的正常語速。一本系統有效的聽力教材，可以使學生通過聽力練習，接觸并逐漸聽懂比他們現有水平略高的語言材料，從而提高學生的自信心，使他們更願意在整個語言學習過程中挑戰自己，形成更積极的語言學習態度。學生通過本書所掌握的聽力策略，不僅有助于他們聽力水平的提高，也有助于閱讀等其它方面能力的提高。

本書每課的聽力訓練都是讓學生先聽大意，再聽細節。"語言點"部分側重于漢語中常見卻又易混淆的表達法和句型。學生可能之前見過這些詞匯或句型，但并不一定能正確使用。通過"語言點"的學習，學生對這些語言點的掌握會得到強化，從而在聽力中有意識地注意這些語言點在具体語境中的使用。二語習得研究表明，明确意識到語言的使用，又稱"注意"，對外語學習而言，至關重要。在教學課程設置中融入本書，教師可以引導學生注意并逐漸适應口語的語言特性，掌握口語中一些語言功能：核實信息、用不同的方式表達相同意思、表示同意或者拒絕、推測、闡釋、猶豫、重复等。這些口語的特殊功用在學生通常接觸的書面漢語中很難見到，它們僅存在于口語中，因為只有在口語中，語言的使用才更具有自發性、隨意性。

語言水平標准

全美外語教學協會(ACTFL)制定的語言標准較詳細地描述了不同層次學生的聽力水平。在本教材的使用上，教師和學生應參照這些標准。下表簡洁闡釋了不同水平的學習者可以完成的聽力任務。

ACTFL 水平	描述
初級中等 (NM)	這一水平的學習者能聽懂一些標準清晰，語境非常具体的簡短詞語。他們能聽懂簡單問句，陳述句和常見指令以及個人信息或肢体行為的慣用語中的一些詞或詞組。這一水平的學生需要講話者講話時留出較長停頓，才能吸收和理解講話的內容。間或學生也會要求講話者重复，或者放慢語速。
初級高等(NH)	這一水平學習者能聽懂一些簡短詞語，以及一些句子，尤其當這些對話的語境十分具体，聲音十分清晰時。他們能聽懂簡單問題，陳述，高頻指示句，以及慣用語。這一水平的學生可能會要求講話者重复，換一种表達方式，或者放慢語速。
中級初等(IL)	這一水平學習者能聽懂一些句子形成的部分話題討論，但是這些句子中的詞匯需要是他們認識的，而且對話語境需要十分清晰。這些話題包括基本個人信息或需要，社交禮儀，日常事物，如買飯，一些基本的指示或說明。聽力任務主要限于自然的、面對面的日常交流。這一水平的學生常常只能斷斷續續聽懂一些內容，可能還需要講話者重复，或者換一种表達方式。常常，他們還是不能完全把握對話的主要內容或某些細節。
中級中等(IM)	這一水平學習者能聽懂一些句子形成的大量話題討論，但句子需要由他們已學詞匯构成。話題內容涵蓋基本個人信息或需要，社交禮儀，以及一些可能更复雜的話題，如住宿、交通、購物。除此之外，他們還能聽懂的話題討論包括個人愛好、活動、以及不同的指示或使用說明。聽力任務不僅包括面對面的自然對話，而且包括一些常見的簡短電話對話，以及一些經過准備的演講，如，媒体的一些簡單聲明、報告。他們能聽懂的信息可能仍然不是連貫的。

ACTFL 水平	描述
中級高等(IH)	這一水平學習者能聽懂在不同時間、不同地點下句群組成的話題討論。他們的聽力可能仍然存在問題，主要障礙在于他們不能完全掌握對話大意或某些細節。換言之，中級高等和高級水平的學習者能聽懂的話題差异不大，但中級高等學習者能聽懂和理解的相對較少。
高級(Adv)	這一水平學習者能聽懂脫离語境之外的較長講話，能理解講話大意以及大多數細節。這一水平學習者的聽力理解可能會受話題熟悉度，語言以及非語言因素等影響。可以聽懂的講話包括不同時態的描述或敘述。可以聽懂熟悉話題相關的采訪、演講、或者事實性的新聞報道。熟悉語言銜接手段，但對如何用這些銜接手段來理解一連串的對話有一定困難。

制定合理目標

聽力的提高是一個循序漸進的過程。有鑒于此，本書鼓勵教師和學生應把使用本書的合理目標定在如何适應這些原汁原味的語言材料，而不應該以百分之百聽懂本書的所有內容做為本書聽力的目標。

教師不必擔心學生無法理解聽力材料中的某些字句，或擔心某些內容太難或太口語化。教師應避免用翻譯的方式講解對話。因為教師如果翻譯了對話內容，學生就沒有机會去适應和理解真實的漢語對話，整個聽力教學也就失去了意義。使用本書時，需要牢記在心的是，聽力教學的目標是讓學生能聽懂真實環境下、未作處理的、常速漢語對話。

學生對本書錄音材料的聽懂程度可能超出教師預料：語言場景會幫助他們理解對話內容，大量練習會讓他們熟悉對話者的聲音。教師不必擔心聽力材料的語速過快。隨着學生聽力提高，他們甚至會感覺這些其實語速相同的對話卻慢了下來。

本書中使用了很多真實的漢語文字道具（如報紙廣告、收据、處方等）。這有利于學生在語言學習初期，就接觸真實地道的漢語文字信息。針對這些語言材料，本書設計的學生任務相對簡單。事實上，本書練習設計的一個重要理念就是讓學生去體會一下"真實漢語"到底是怎樣的。熟悉目標語的文化，是外語學習中的一項重要目標。而用真實語言材料，正有助于學生文化意識的培養。

《溝通》与教學課程設置

《溝通》并不适合用作漢語教學的核心教材。本書的語法講解相對零散，基本不包含漢語閱讀。這些方面的漢語知識應主要來自核心教材。本教材需要的備課時間較少。教師只需課前稍事准備，就可在講解核心教材時，穿插使用本書中的練習。盡管教師可以按照本書聽力與核心教材的話題匹配來設置課堂教學，這种搭配方式卻并非最理想的。教師需要首先考慮學生的實際語言水平，從而選擇本教材中与學生語言水平相差不大的部分作為教學內容，而非僅從本教材与核心教材的話題匹配度上來設置您的教學。配套語音材料中的對話，在情節上是逐漸發展的，如果能保持這些內容的連貫性，學生會更感興趣。如果教師在選擇時隨意性過大，這一連貫性則被打斷，學生做聽力的興趣可能會有所降低。

本書第1–23課話題順序和《中文聽說讀寫》第一級中的話題順序基本一致。注意《溝通》（第二版）與《中文聽說讀寫》（第三版）的話題順序有些出入。在講解《中文聽說讀寫》中每一課的新話題時，建議不要同時使用本書。因本書側重于幫學生復習鞏固已有知識，而非介紹新知。盡管《溝通》是《中文聽說讀寫》的絕佳搭配，但本書也可与其他綜合教材配合使用，重點幫助學生提高聽力水平。對已有一定的漢語背景知識的漢語自學者或華裔學生來說，本書也可以作為聽力教材單獨使用，專攻學生聽力水平。

本書主要适合于初級中等(NM)到初級高等水平(NH)的漢語學生。使用本書時，學生已經學過本書中的相應話題。他們可通過本書的聽力訓練，復習之前已學的語言文化知識。由于本書中新語言點的出現和使用非常少，使用本書時不必擔心本書中的語言知識會影響學生的整体漢語學習進度。

聽力教學不需要占用太多課堂時間，大多數聽力練習都可以以家庭作業或网上任務的形式完成。

溫故知新

語言學習無法一蹴而就。學生需要反复練習從而鞏固提高已學的知識。這一理念在時下的一些教科書中已有所体現，但反复使用同一類型的教材會讓學生感到枯燥無聊，初級高等（NH）到中級低等(IL)的學生尤其會感到如此。

本書貫穿的兩條二語習得原則：

- 詞匯需要不斷復習和回顧以使之存儲于學生的長期記憶里。
- 詞匯及語言點需要以不同形式出現

在二語教學中，教師通常很重視新材料的學習，卻忽視了以上兩條重要原則的教學意義。《溝通》通過真實自然的聲音材料，系統回顧并加強學生對已學話題的理解，同時本書也着重訓練學生的聽力技巧，提高學生聽力水平。本書的話題對學生而言，都是舊話題，但通過本書，學生可以在全新的、生動的語言環境下對這些舊的詞匯、語法點有新的認識。本書每課都包含少量新材料，教學主要目標是掌握書中明确標識的重要語言點。其他核心教材可以給學生提供新材料，而本書則可以給學生一种相對更自由，更發散的外語學習經歷。學生有更多的机會復習舊知識和接觸新知識，從而對這些知識點由概念性理解，到部分理解，直至完全理解（參見下圖）：

語言教學的連貫和銜接

常常一個漢語班上的學生背景迥異，語言程度參差不齊。本書作為輔助教材，將學生已學詞匯、語言點恰當的融入在不同的練習中。使用本書，有利於不同水平的學生根據自己需要，個性化自己的學習過程。學生可以根據自己水平，決定同一段錄音需要聽几次。《溝通》是連接不同水平核心語言課教材的一座橋梁。它的作用不可忽視。語言學習過程并非完全連續、毫無間隔。學習過程中是存在一些空檔期的，如寒、暑假等。這些間隔對語言學習產生的影響需要通過相應教材的使用得到改善。在從初級到中級，再到高級的語言學習過程中，不同年級的教學之間應該做到高度銜接，從而促進學生持續不斷的吸收知識，提高能力。僅依賴于某一本或某一套教材，可能并不能使學生完全達到預期的外語水平量化指標。

增強學生學習動力

不同學生的學習進度不盡相同。初級中等(NH)至中級中等(IL)程度的學生尤其需要聽力強化訓練。本書為不同水平學生搭建了一個共同的平台，以降低學生外語學習恐懼，增強學習動力，從而創造出一個良性的外語學習環境。

接觸"真實"漢語，比完全依賴課本文字材料的講解，會讓學生覺得有更多互動，更有趣。盡管本書錄音材料可能有一定難度，但本書向學生展示了真實的漢語對話究竟如何（母語人士也會支支吾吾！）。由于本書循序漸進的課程設置，隨着學生所聽對話的增多，他們理解對話的能力和信心都會加倍增長。這种成就感將极大的增強他們的外語學習動力，從而促進學生整体漢語水平和交際能力的提高。

包容語言多樣性

正如任何其他語言，漢語教師和學生要充分認識到漢語使用的多樣性。錄音中的獨白或對話中可能存在語音語法"錯誤"，錄音中的表達法與其他教材，或任課老師的習慣用法可能不盡一致。盡管本書中所有錄音均來自漢語母語人士，但他們的語言中無可避免的包含一些不盡"正確"之處。作為教師，我們不必擔心這些不同的用法會對學生外語學習產生消极影

響 — 這僅表明語言使用存在差异。事實上，學生也需要在學習語言之初就認識到語言使用的這一特征。當今，受各种媒体以及互聯網的影響，跨國旅行的便捷，國外留學机會的增多，某一語言現象的使用也越來越不僅局限于某一地域。若本書錄音中某些語言使用，或發音尤其少見，本書在附注中會給予說明。教師可以通過指出某詞匯更常用于中國大陸還是台灣地區，說明兩者差異。同樣，本書使用的廣告，通知等文字樣本，有些來源于大陸地區，有些來源于台灣地區。通過這些差異，學生可以更直觀的領略到語言使用的多樣化。從這點上講，本書有利于學生完成從教室漢語到眞實漢語的過渡。

每課聽力的設置

《溝通》以圖式理論為教學模型，每一課都由五部分組成。以聽前熱身開始，其目的在于提供相關背景材料。以輸出性技能訓練結束，其目的在于幫助學生把錄音中所聽到的詞匯和句型運用到自己的口語和寫作中。

第一步　熱身

在每一課的正式聽力練習前，學生首先需要對即將進行的聽力話題有所了解。熱身階段的第一部分列出了該課聽力材料用到的相關詞匯。在詞匯學習上，本書盡量多的使用圖畫形式引入詞匯：本書設計了圖文匹配練習，這道題要求學生將生字、生詞（部分附有拼音）和圖片進行匹配。本書也為生詞提供了簡短解釋。根据課程的難度，解釋有時用漢語，有時用英語。此外，對于比較地道的固定表達，本書還提供了例句。

研究表明，聽前准備時，激活學生已有知識（心理圖式）有助于他們聽懂相關對話。熱身階段的第二部分通常是聽前准備活動。這一部分可用于課堂討論（教師可以根据學生程度決定討論是用英語還是漢語）。聽前准備幫助學生對將聽材料的背景有一定了解。新對話中的詞匯或概念在聽前練習題中出現，有利于學生對將聽的材料做好准備。這一部分專門提供了"便箋"，主要用于讓學生做筆記或者記錄一些問題的答案（學生可以自由選擇用英語還是漢語做筆記。教師不應讓學生上交這部分內容，或對學生的"便箋"進行評分）。除此之外，另外一個在線腦力激蕩平台Bubbl.us(https://bubbl.us/)也很有用。

第二步　泛聽

現在學生要開始聽第一遍聽力材料了。在聽之前，他們應該先看看聽力問題。這樣，在正式聽的時候，他們就會知道哪些信息更需要關注。在泛聽階段，聽力任務逐漸引導學生了解聽力材料的基本信息，比如，對話者之間是何种關系，對話在哪里發生，對話大概講了什么。這部分練習不多，而且相對容易。練習的主要目的在于讓學生宏觀理解錄音材料。如果學生覺得困難，可以再聽一次。這部分練習最好是在課堂內完成。

第三步　靜聽

精聽階段的練習主要是任務型的。這部分練習要求學生聽懂較多信息，學生需要回答對話者究竟講了什麼，如何講之類的問題。練習類型包括圖表完成題，選擇題，正誤判斷，搭配，以及完形填空。根據題目難度不同，有些題目使用全英文提問，有些則是使用漢英結合的方式提問。第三階段應該在課堂外完成，這樣學生可以根據自己需要，決定相關錄音需要聽的次數。

第四步　語言點

一旦學生了解對話的大致內容，老師要引導學生將注意力重點放在詞匯使用，語言運用，以及句型等語言知識上。這一階段的練習題包括詞匯搭配、完成對話、完成句子、完形填空、翻譯以及選擇題。錄音中出現的語言點并未在練習題中一一出現，練習題的目的在于強調少部分尤其重要的語言只是。盡管學生已經學過這些語言點，這部分練習將有利于學生復習和鞏固相關知識。這一部分練習題也适合在課外完成，學生可以根據自己需要，決定相關錄音需要聽的次數。

第五步　應用

第五步主要用來訓練學生口語與寫作能力。每一課的口語與寫作練習都与該課已聽過的對話有關。題目類型有角色扮演、完成對話、以及寫作。這些題目既可以用于課堂教學，也可以用于自學。題目的設計也很靈活，教師和學生可以根據需要做相應變動。寫作或者口語練習可以很方便的上載到网站，這樣全班可以相互學習。這种全班分享的模式比教師教、學生學的模式更互動，更有利于激發學生學習動力，提高學生外語輸出能力。

本書目錄

本書所有獨白或對話均未經過事先演練。錄音者講話時并無草稿，錄音中使用的詞匯也未經限制。換言之，本書錄音時力求語言模擬真實。本書每課都提供了寫作練習題目。下表標明了本書課文難度和ACTFL水平的關系。

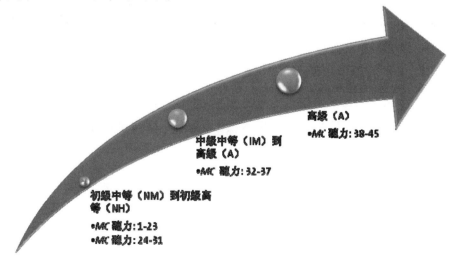

高級（A）
•MC 獨力: 38-45

中級中等（IM）到
高級（A）
•MC 聽力: 32-37

初級中等（NM）到初級高
等（NH）
•MC 聽力: 1-23
•MC 聽力: 24-31

　　需要注意的是，盡管本書聽力32-45課錄音材料的語言程度看似高于您學生的現有水平，但事實卻可能并非如此。通過1-31課的學習，學生會掌握一些聽力策略。而第二部分的練習題會引導學生使用這些策略，從而理解32-45課的錄音材料。另外，學生不必聽懂每一個詞，每一個細節。本書聽力練習題有意融入了一些學生之前可能學過，也可能沒學過的詞匯和表達法。這一策略有益于學生接觸和掌握比他們現有水平略高的語言材料。學生可以通過練習題中提供的一些背景，或其他線索推測對話中的內容，從而聽懂比他們現有水平略高的錄音材料。這也是本書與其他常規中文教材的一個重要區別，其他教材的生詞或句型可能僅來源于學校漢語，或者僅包括標准漢語，而本書卻非如此。在使用本書時，學生一開始可能感覺自己的進步不明顯，或者聽力材料太難，但不久，他們就會發現通過練習，自己可以在眞實中文環境中更好的交流。24-45課尤其适合于打算出國或想繼續學習高級水平漢語的學生。

第一部分：1-23課

　　這部分的話題順序與《中文聽說讀寫》第一級的話題順序基本一致。注意《溝通》（第二版）與《中文聽說讀寫》（第三版）的話題順序有些出入。盡管《溝通》是《中文聽說讀寫》的絕佳搭配，但這并非本書使用的唯一方式。本書亦可作為獨立的聽力教材，和其他綜合漢語教材搭配使用。如果您在自學漢語，或是華裔學生，具有一定的漢語背景知識，本書可以幫助您專門強化聽力。

第二部分：24-45課

　　學生在學習完第一部分大部分內容之后，會比較熟悉本書每課的編排模式，聽力重點。此時他們的程度正好适合更具多樣性的第二部分。第一部分中的材料基本都是同樣的兩人對話；第二部分的錄音來源則更廣泛，學生可以有机會感受不同說話者的語音，也可以了解更丰富的對話內容。大部分的對話或獨白的場景都設定在美國；有6課（第24-28課，以及第31課）錄音是以中國為背景的；另外有3課（第40，41，45課）可能取材自中國或台灣之外的漢語廣播。跟第一部分一樣，第二部分的講話者也都是自然語速，未經准備。

　　本書最后八課的語言程度和ACTFL优异水平(Superior)接近，對向這一水平邁進的學生而言，這些聽力課程，既是一項挑戰，也是一种資源。這八課錄音材料中有几位說話者有些許口音，語法使用也非完美。這些錄音材料給學生了一個接觸非標准漢語的机會，因為他們在今后的漢語學習過程中，必然會遇見非標準漢語使用的情況。教師應該對這些非標准漢語的使用持寬容態度，避免過分強調標准漢語應該如何表達。如果放手讓學生去專注該課的教學重點，他們會從這些不同的漢語使用中獲得更大受益。

　　本書聽取更喜歡在漢語環境下學漢語的教師和學生的建議，在24-45課的一些難度較高的聽力課文的對應練習題中使用了更多的漢語。

對教材使用的建議

模式一：配合《中文聽說讀寫》初中級教材

對已經學完大學第一學期中文或相當于此的學生：（配合教材《中文聽說讀寫》第一級的第2部分為例），本書中第一部分1-23課的內容可以作為補充教材，每星期教一課。對已經上完大學一學年中文或相當于此的學生：（以配合教材《中文聽說讀寫》第二級為例），本書1-23課的內容可以作為補充教材，在學期開始可以每星期使用1-3課。

課堂上：每次課結束前10分鐘。

教師可以和學生一起完成聽力前的活動。教師應根據學生的語言水平選擇用中文或英文進行這部分練習。學生可以是多人小組或兩人一組活動。每課的"第一步"將向學生介紹本課內容中的生詞。完成這步后，教師可以引導學生讀"泛聽"部分的練習題目。接下來，教師播放相應聽力材料一次或兩次。播放過程中不要暫停。每次播放完后，可以适當留几分鐘讓學生回答書上的聽力問題。

家庭作業

學生可以在家完成每課"第三步"、"第四步"中的練習題目（他們需要有本書的錄音）。作業完成后交給教師批改。

課堂上：跟進（可以用半堂課的時間）

這一環節可以安排在每周課程的后半部分：理想的情況是在學生交了他們的家庭 作業之后。"第五步"中的口語活動非常适合在課堂完成。額外的詞語或語法的練習，教師如認為有必要，也可以同時融入課堂。"第五步"的口語或寫作練習特別适合作為家庭作業。這些作業都可以放在校內的网站上，便于在學生和老師內部交流。

模式二：對已經完成兩個學年大學課程的大學生

在每個新學年開始的時候，可以用第一部分聽力材料做密集練習。學生應該有能力獨立完成大部分的內容。寫作部分的練習可以每星期交一次，或收集在一個文件夾里。

在余下的學年里，對第二部分中的作業分配可以和第一部分大致相同（每周或每兩周完成一課聽力）。理想狀態下，教師應按照模式一中所列的步驟來安排每課進程（如，在做對話練習之前先完成"熱身活動"）。如此，教師和學生都會深感聽力在整個中文教學中的重要性。教師可根據學生的實際程度決定使用第二部分中的哪些材料。大多數學生在聽完之前的聽力后都可以接受24-31課的聽力難度。32-45課對應ACTFL高級水平(A),部分老師可能會認為這部分課程更适合留給三、四年級，或喜歡做有挑戰性練習的學生使用。

司馬德琳

2012年1月

Abbreviations

Adj	adjective
Adv	adverb
Coll	colloquial
Conj	conjunction
MW	measure word
N	noun
Nu	number
Ph	phrase
PRC	People's Republic of China usage
Prep	preposition
Suf	suffix
TW	Taiwan usage
V	verb
V O	verb-object

Preparation 熱身

Useful Vocabulary

系	xì	N	department (e.g. 英文系, 中文系, 歷史系)
前	qián	N	(前頭 qiántou / 前面 qiánmian)
後	hòu	N	(後頭 / 後面)
上	shàng	N	(上面)
下	xià	N	(下面)
旁邊	pángbiān	N	side
東	dōng	N	(東邊)
南	nán	N	(南邊)
西	xī	N	(西邊)
北	běi	N	(北邊)
對面	duìmiàn	N	opposite, right in front of
正好	zhènghǎo	Adv	just right; by a happy coincidence, it just turns out that, by chance, as it turns out
Example:			
小張正好也要去中文系。			
咱們	zánmen	N	we (including speaker; this usage occurs in northern dialects)

See if you can locate these places on the map above and say what parts of China they are in:

吉林 *Jílín*　　　　北京 *Běijīng*　　　　上海 *Shànghǎi*

長春 *Chángchūn*　　香港 *Xiānggǎng*　　西寧 *Xīníng*
　　　　　　　　　　　　(Hong Kong)

Example:

吉林 *Jílín* 在中國的東北。

▶ Listening for the Gist 泛聽

Listen to the dialogue. Check which places are mentioned:

❑ Beijing　　　❑ Changchun

❑ Shanghai　　❑ Hong Kong

❑ Taipei

The people in this dialogue are:

- ❏ a Chinese tourist and a teacher of Chinese
- ❏ two Chinese students from the PRC (People's Republic of China)
- ❏ two Chinese teachers from the PRC
- ❏ a Chinese student from Taiwan and a Chinese student from the PRC

The person who is asking for directions is:

- ❏ female   ❏ male

This conversation takes place:

- ❏ on a college campus   ❏ at the airport
- ❏ at a bookstore   ❏ at a bus station

▶ Listening for Details 靜聽

The woman's name is: (circle one)

Li Yingwen   Li Wenyang

Li Wenyin   Li Wenying

Based on the information given, see if you can write the rest of her name in characters:

李_____

The man's name is: (circle one)

Zhang Linshen   Zhang Linsheng

Zhang Lingshen   Zhang Lingsheng

Based on the information given, see if you can write the rest of his name in characters:

張_____

The woman is asking directions to:

- ❏ the Department of English
- ❏ the Department of Chinese
- ❏ a Chinese restaurant
- ❏ the library

The person who gives directions has lived in the United States for:

❑　three years　　❑　five years

❑　four years　　❑　six years

Key Language Points 語言點

Zhang Linsheng and Li Wenying were talking about how American campuses were laid out differently from Chinese campuses. He happened to have a map of Beijing University and was showing it to Li Wenying. A small part of this map has been reproduced on the following page. Indicate whether the following statements are true (是) or false (非). A gloss to some of the place names is given below.

未名	wèi míng	unnamed
湖	hú	lake
樓	lóu	building
哲學	zhéxué	philosophy
體育館	tǐyùguǎn	gymnasium
教室	jiàoshì	classroom
生物(學)	shēngwù(xué)	biology
地(理)學	dìlǐxué	geography
文史	wénshǐ	literature and history
化學	huàxué	chemistry

圖書館在未名湖的西邊。　　　　　　　　　　是　非

哲學樓在第二體育館旁邊。　　　　　　　　　是　非

第一教室樓的後面是生物北館。　　　　　　是　非

地學樓在文史樓跟化學樓的中間。　　　　　是　非

第一體育館正好在第二體育館對面。　　　　是　非

文史樓前頭就是地學樓。 是 非

未名湖離第一體育館不遠。 是 非

圖書館旁邊沒有教室。 是 非

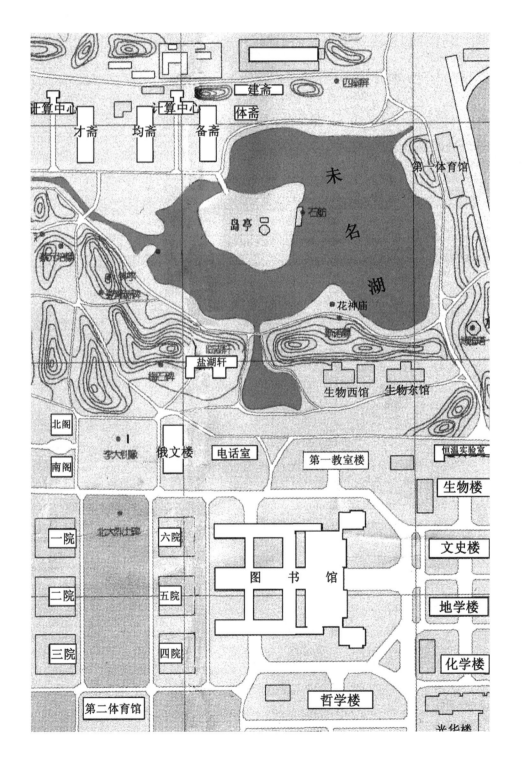

Complete the following short paragraph using words or expressions from the following list:

高興　　剛　　認識　　好像　　中文系　　正好　　英文系

小李跟小張以前不 _____。他們兩個人都是 _____ 的研究生 (yánjiūshēng, yánjiùshēng: graduate students)。小李 _____ 到美國，_____ 她有一點寂寞 (jímò, jìmò: lonely)。今天她 _____ 看到了小張，所以她現在很 _____。

Follow-up Activities 應用

大家來説 Role-Playing (Oral)

With a partner practice introducing yourself in Chinese. Be sure to explain how to write your name. Below is a sample dialogue you might want to use as a guide. First take turns reading this dialogue aloud.

王：我姓王，叫王友生。

高：王先生，你好! 你的名字怎麼寫?

王：友就是朋友的友。生是醫生的生。

高：這個名字真好聽! 我姓高，我叫高英美。

王："Ying" 是什么 "Ying"?

高："Ying" 是英國的英，"Mei" 是美國的美。

王：高小姐，認識你很高興!

高：認識你也很高興。

王：你是什麼地方來的？

高：我是台北來的。你呢？

王：我是上海來的。

大家來寫 **Role-Playing (Written)**

Referring to the map, identify the name of the province (give the Chinese characters and pīnyīn) in which these cities can be found.

長沙 Chángshā

_____

天津 Tiānjīn

_____

昆明 Kūnmíng

_____

上海 Shànghǎi

_____

成都 Chéngdū

_____

青海 Qīnghǎi

_____

西安 Xī'ān

_____

長春 Chángchūn

_____

武漢 Wǔhàn

_____

哈爾濱 Hāěrbīn

_____

Preparation 熱身

Useful Vocabulary

非常	fēicháng	Adv	extraordinarily, very
全	quán	Adv	all, completely
主要	zhǔyào	Adj	for the most part, main, chief
理解	lǐjiě	V	to understand (cf. 懂)

See if you can guess the meaning of these words from the way they are used in the following sentences:

退休 tuìxiū 剛 gāng

我爸爸今年六十五歲了，他大概 (dàgài: probably) 會退休。

張林生剛來美國的時候非常想家，慢慢兒就好起來了。

Think of times when you feel homesick (xiǎngjiā 想家). What do you do to cheer yourself up? Do you think these feelings of homesickness would be different for a student from China? Why or why not? Take a few minutes to jot down some of these thoughts or share them with a partner in class.

_____

_____

_____

_____

_____

▶ Listening for the Gist 泛聽

Why did Zhang Linsheng initiate this conversation?

❑ He had a question about coursework he wanted to ask Ms. Li.

❑ He could tell Ms. Li was unhappy.

❑ He wanted to tell Ms. Li about his family.

❑ He wanted to ask Ms. Li to have dinner.

Why is Li Wenying feeling homesick?

❑ She just got a phone call from her parents.

❑ She was looking at a picture of her daughter.

❑ She just received a letter from home.

❑ All her classmates have activities planned for the weekend.

Circle the members of Li Wenying and Zhang Linsheng's families that are mentioned in this conversation.*

Li	Zhang
grandparents	grandparents
father	father
mother	mother
younger brother	younger brother
older brother	older brother
younger sister	younger sister
older sister	older sister
husband	wife
daughter	daughter
son	son

*NOTE: When Zhang Linsheng talks about his family, he doesn't need to use the possessive marker 的, since it is generally omitted when referring to close family members. Similarly, it is not necessary to include a measure word when referring to someone's occupation, i.e., Zhang Linsheng could have said, "我妹妹是工人。"

▶ Listening for Details 靜聽

Check all the members of Li Wenying's family that she mentions, then draw a line connecting each of them to their occupation in Column B.

Column A	Column B
grandparents	teacher
father	lawyer
mother	is retired
younger brother	doctor
older brother	worker
younger sister	college student
older sister	high school student
husband	

Where are Li Wenying's family members now living? (circle all that apply)

United States   Beijing   Harbin

Shanghai   Changchun   Nanjing

How old is Li Wenying's daughter?

☐ 一歲   ☐ 四歲   ☐ 兩歲   ☐ 她沒說   ☐ 三歲

Now listen to what Zhang Linsheng says about his family and then use the table on the following page to draw a line connecting each family member he mentions to their occupation in Column B.

Column A	Column B
grandparents	teacher
father	lawyer
mother	is retired
younger brother	doctor
older brother	worker
younger sister	college student
older sister	high school student
wife	

Why does Li Wenying thank Zhang Linsheng at the end of the conversation?

- ❑ Because talking to him cheered her up.
- ❑ Because he gave her some good ideas about how to cheer herself up.
- ❑ Because he invited her to meet his family.
- ❑ Because he showed her pictures of his family.

Key Language Points 語言點

Below are two frequently used idiomatic expressions that occurred in this dialogue. See if you can translate the following examples into English.

怪不得   guàibudé   "no wonder"

就是說   jiùshìshuō   "that is to say . . ." (used for clarification or explanation)

Examples:

甲：你的中文怎麼説得那麼好？

乙：我從小就在家裡説中文。

甲：怪不得。

甲：你的意思就是説，中文是你的母語 ("mother tongue": native language) 對不對？

乙：對，可以這樣説。

Complete these two dialogues using either 怪不得 or 就是説. Then translate them into English.

李：我今天非常想家。

張：爲什麽？

李：因爲我家裡的人剛給我打電話了。

張：＿＿＿＿＿＿＿你有一點不高興。

_____

_____

張：你弟弟做什麼工作？

李：他又是學生，又是老師。

張：這是什麼意思？

李：這＿＿＿＿＿＿＿他大學還没畢業 (bìyè: to graduate)，所以還不能當 (dāng: to act as) 眞正 (zhēnzhèng: real, true) 的老師。

張：啊，我懂了。

_____

_____

Follow-up Activities 應用

大家來說 Role-Playing (Oral)

With a partner, find out about each other's family. For example, you could ask how many brothers and sisters s/he has,* how old they are, what they do, where they live, how often s/he calls or writes them. Be sure to use the expressions 怪不得 and 就是說.

*HINT: the general term for brothers and sisters is 兄弟姐妹 (xiōngdì jiěmèi).

大家來寫 **Role-Playing (Written)**

Later that night Li Wenying decided to write a letter to her family. Can you help her complete it?

收到(shōudào: received) 你們的信以後，我心裡 _____ 。

我來美國已經 _____ 月了，可是_____ 。

你們最近好嗎？弟弟 _____ ？爸爸的身體

(shēntǐ: lit. "body" health) _____ ？

媽媽的 _____

_____ ？

希望你們常常給我寫 _____ 。

祝

_____

文英　　　上

_____年_____月_____日

Preparation 熱身

Useful Vocabulary

挺好	tǐng hǎo	Adv	很好
感謝	gǎnxiè	Adv	非常謝謝一個人 (often used in formal speech or written contexts)

Review these expressions—write down a situation (in English) when each could be used.

不(用)謝

_____

不(用)客氣

_____

哪裡哪裡

_____

沒有什麼

_____

沒事(兒)

_____

那也可以

_____

What do you like to do to celebrate your birthday? List three things.

_____

_____

_____

Do you think Chinese attitudes toward celebrating birthdays are different from those of Americans? In what ways? Why do Chinese (especially older people) often eat noodles on their birthdays?

_____

_____

_____

_____

_____

_____

_____

▶ Listening for the Gist 泛聽

Listen to the conversation and check which of these expressions you hear.

	✓
不用謝	
不用客氣	
哪裡哪裡	
沒有什麼	
沒事(兒)*	
那也可以	
感謝	
你太客氣了	

*People from Northern China (especially Beijing) often add 兒 ér endings. If you listen closely, you'll notice that Zhang Linsheng, who is from Beijing, sometimes pronounces words in this way.

▶ Listening for Details 靜聽

How did Li Wenying find out when Zhang Linsheng's birthday is?

- ❑ From his wife
- ❑ From his daughter
- ❑ From a mutual friend
- ❑ She saw the date on his passport

Zhang Linsheng's birthday is on (circle one):

Mon.   Tues.   Wed.   Thurs.   Fri.   Sat.   Sun.

What is the date of his birthday?

- ❑ June 29
- ❑ September 26
- ❑ June 26
- ❑ September 29

What kind of food do they decide to eat?

❏ Chinese   ❏ Korean

❏ American   ❏ Japanese

❏ Thai

What time do they decide to meet?

❏ 6:00 p.m.

❏ 6:30 p.m.

❏ 7:00 p.m.

❏ 7:30 p.m.

Where is the restaurant located?

❏ Next to her house

❏ Next to his house

❏ Across the street from her house

❏ Across the street from his house

Key Language Points 語言點

Which of the responses best answers the following questions? Check all that are appropriate.

你最近怎麼樣？ (Nǐ zuìjìn zěnme yàng?)

❏ 很忙   ❏ 好玩   ❏ 挺好

❏ 很快   ❏ 不錯

你找我有事嗎？ (Nǐ zhǎo wǒ yǒu shì ma?)

❏ 我想吃美國飯。   ❏ 我想請你們全家去吃飯。

❏ 我想請你幫我的忙。   ❏ 我想謝謝你。

Below are some phrases that generally would elicit a polite response. Which of the expressions would be best to say in each situation? Sometimes more than one response will work. Check all that apply.

	不用謝	不用客氣	哪裡哪裡
因爲和你聊天，我現在舒服多了。			
你眞是一個好人。			
我想好好感謝你一下。			
我要請你去吃飯。			
你做的菜非常好吃。			
謝謝你幫助我學中文。			
你的中國話説得挺好。			

*NOTE: Remember that 幫助 can be a verb or a noun, whereas 幫忙 is always a verb+object. So when Li Wenying says, "你給了我不少幫忙," she made a grammatical mistake. What should she have said?

Follow-up Activities 應用

大家來説 Role-Playing (Oral)

A. After hanging up the phone, Zhang Linsheng told his wife about his conversation with Li Wenying. She suggested that they eat later, since she has to work late that evening. "Recreate" this conversation with a partner.

B. Later that evening Zhang Linsheng called Li Wenying back again to revise their plans. "Recreate" this conversation with a partner.

大家來寫 **Role-Playing (Written)**

Zhang Linsheng wrote a note to his wife telling her about the plans he had made with Li Wenying. What might this note say?

_____

_____

_____

_____

_____

_____

_____

_____

_____

Preparation 熱身

Useful Vocabulary

玩(玩兒)	wán (wár)	V	to have fun, to enjoy, to play

Examples:

See if you can translate these sentences into English. Pay special attention to each usage of 玩 (玩兒).

1. 小張覺得周末應該去玩一玩。
2. 踢足球很好玩。
3. 小張也喜歡玩電腦。(diànnǎo: computer)
4. 他告訴他的美國朋友，北京可以玩的地方很多。

原來	yuánlái	Adv	1. previously, in the past, originally 2. it turns out that, as it turns out

Examples:

1. 原來你在中國的時候喜歡玩什麼呢？

What did you used to like to do for fun when you were in China?

2. 李文英原來不會游泳，怪不得她不想到海邊去。

It turns out that Li Wenying doesn't know how to swim. No wonder she doesn't want to go to the beach.

輕鬆	qīngsōng	Adj	relaxed
活動	huódòng	N	activities

Talk to your class/partner about what you each like to do in your free time. Do you think these activities would be different if you were studying abroad? In what ways?

_____

_____

_____

_____

_____

_____

_____

▶ Listening for the Gist 泛聽

Which of these topics is mentioned in this conversation? (check all that apply)

❑ What Xiao Li is studying

❑ Kinds of movies Xiao Li likes to see

❑ Kinds of sports Xiao Zhang likes to play

❑ The idea of "weekend" in the U.S. and China

❑ Chinese movies versus American movies

❑ Activities that Xiao Li used to do in China

❑ Activities that Xiao Zhang used to do in China

❑ Activities that Xiao Li does in the U.S.

❑ Activities that Xiao Zhang does in the U.S.

In this conversation, who suggests that they do something together? (circle one)

李文英   張林生

What does s/he suggest they do?

_____

_____

▶ Listening for Details 靜聽

Where do you think this conversation takes place?

❑ At the library   ❑ At the recreation center

❑ Outside a movie theater   ❑ At a bus stop

What day of the week is it? (circle one)

Monday   Tuesday   Wednesday   Thursday

Friday   Saturday   Sunday

What time of day is it? (circle one)

morning   noontime   afternoon   evening

Check all the activities that Li Wenying says she used to do for fun when she was in China.

❑ Go to the movies   ❑ Watch television

❑ Sing   ❑ Read

❑ Go out to eat   ❑ Visit friends

❑ Listen to music   ❑ Go swimming

❑ Go dancing   ❑ Sleep

Check all the activities that Zhang Linsheng says he does for fun.

❑ Go to the movies   ❑ Watch television

❑ Go dancing   ❑ Play football

❑ Go out to eat   ❑ Visit friends

❑ Listen to music   ❑ Go swimming

❑ Sleep   ❑ Play ping pong

Based on the dialogue, complete the chart:

Day	
Time movie starts	
Time they will meet	
Place where they will meet	
Who else will go to the movies with them	

How does Zhang Linsheng say *Star Wars* in Chinese?

❏ 星星大戰　xīngxing dàzhàn

❏ 星球戰爭　xīngqiú zhànzhēng

❏ 星球大戰　xīngqiú dàzhàn

❏ 星星戰爭　xīngxing zhànzhēng

Key Language Points 語言點

Choose the verb that goes with each of these objects; in some cases there may be two verbs that are correct. Also, each verb may be used more than once.

唱　打　念　看　跳　吃　聽　睡　喝

Example: _____ 飯　=　___吃___ 飯

_____ 電影　　_____ 舞

_____ 音樂　　_____ 球

_____ 書　　_____ 歌

_____ 水果　　_____ 電視

_____ 覺　　_____ 汽水

Practice using 原來 yuánlái.

Usage #1. Rewrite the following sentences using 原來⋯後來⋯

Example:

張林生找不到李文英。李文英在圖書館看書。

↳ 張林生原來找不到李文英，後來才在圖書館看到她。

1. 李文英來美國以前不喜歡吃美國飯。現在她覺得美國飯很好吃。

_____

_____

2. 張林生去年常常帶他女兒去玩。今年他特別 (tèbié: especially) 忙，又得教書(jiāoshū: to teach)又得上課。

_____

_____

3. 小李的先生上高中的時候住在北京。他上大學以後住在長春。

_____

_____

Usage #2. Based on the situations described above, use 原來 meaning "it turns out that" to complete these sentences.

Example:

李文英下午不在家，

↳　原來在圖書館看書＿＿＿＿＿＿＿＿＿＿＿＿＿＿＿＿＿＿＿＿。

1. 小李在中國吃了美國飯。

原來＿＿＿＿＿＿＿＿＿＿＿＿＿＿＿＿＿＿＿＿＿＿＿＿。

2. 張林生今年很少帶他女兒去玩，

原來是因為＿＿＿＿＿＿＿＿＿＿＿＿＿＿＿＿＿＿＿＿。

3. 我以為小李的先生住在北京，

原來＿＿＿＿＿＿＿＿＿＿＿＿＿＿＿＿＿＿＿＿＿＿＿＿。

Follow-up Activities 應用

大家來說 Role-Playing (Oral)

Below are newspaper clippings about several movies that are showing. Decide with a partner what movie you will see, then decide on which showing, where you will meet, and what time you will meet.

大家來寫 **Role-Playing (Written)**

Write a brief essay describing what you do on the weekends and during the week. Include at least five of the activities depicted in the pictures below.

Preparation 熱身

Identify the following beverages using the appropriate Chinese characters:

茶 chá   可樂 kělè   汽水 qìshuǐ   牛奶 niúnǎi

果汁 guǒzhī   啤酒 píjiǔ   咖啡 kāfēi

水   shuǐ (also called 開水* kāishuǐ or 白開水 báikāishuǐ)

*NOTE: kāi is "boiled" here. Keep in mind that people don't drink tap water in China.

Additional Useful Vocabulary

待一會兒	dài yì huǐ(r)	Coll	等一會兒 děng yì huǐ(r), in a little bit, in a short while (cf. děng yí xià 等一下)
聊天	liáotiān	V	説話
習慣	xíguàn	V	to grow accustomed to
		N	a habit

Examples: See if you can translate these sentences into English.

小李不習慣天天喝咖啡。

_____

她也没有喝啤酒的習慣。

_____

流行	liúxíng	Adj/V	to be popular, to be trendy (refers to inanimate objects or abstract ideas, never to people)

Examples: See if you can translate these sentences into English.

最近很流行穿黑色的衣服。

_____

中國人現在流行看美國電影。

_____

▶ Listening for the Gist 泛聽

Where do you think Xiao Li and Xiao Zhang have just returned from?

❏ A movie theater

❏ Another classmate's dorm room

❏ School

❏ A video store

Where does most of this conversation take place?

- ❏ At Xiao Li's apartment
- ❏ In the car
- ❏ At Xiao Zhang's apartment
- ❏ In another classmate's dorm room

▶ Listening for Details 靜聽

How many times has Xiao Zhang's daughter seen this movie?

- ❏ Once
- ❏ Twice
- ❏ Three times
- ❏ Four times

What comments does Xiao Li make about Xiao Zhang's apartment? (check all that apply)

- ❏ It is large.
- ❏ It is new.
- ❏ It is clean.
- ❏ He has a lot of books.
- ❏ He has a good selection of music.

Which of the following does Xiao Zhang offer her to drink? (check all that apply)

- ❏ Tea
- ❏ Juice
- ❏ Coffee
- ❏ Soda
- ❏ Beer
- ❏ Water

Write what she decides to drink in Chinese characters.

_____

Where is Xiao Zhang's wife?

- ❏ At work
- ❏ At the store
- ❏ At school
- ❏ At the library

What does Xiao Zhang suggest they do . . .

	. . . before his wife returns?	. . . after his wife returns?
Have something to drink.		
Have a snack to eat.		
Listen to music.		
Watch TV.		
Look at books.		
Chat.		
Prepare 餃子 (jiǎozi) for dinner.		
Play with his daughter.		

Which of the following expressions did Xiao Zhang and Xiao Li use to describe the movie? (circle all that apply)

非常有意思　　挺好　　不太好　　不錯　　很無聊 (wúliáo: boring)

沒有意思　　很好　　很流行　　非常幽默 (yōumò: humorous)

Key Language Points 語言點

Do you remember the difference between 有意思, 沒有意思, 不好意思, and . . . 的意思? See if you can fill in the blanks below with the appropriate expression. Then translate the paragraph into idiomatic English.

看完了電影，小張請小李來他家吃飯。張太太還沒回來，所以小李有一點 _____。小張的書非常多，除了中文書以外，還有英文書和日文書。小李覺得這些書都很 _____，可是她不懂日文書名 _____。因爲小張覺得看電視 _____ 所以他們兩個人就一邊聊天，一邊等張太太回來。

_____

_____

_____

_____

_____

_____

_____

_____

* * *

Fill in the blanks using an expression from the list below.

不過   流行   待(一)會兒   習慣   聊天   等等

1. 小李不 _____ 美國的生活。(shēnghuó: life)

2. 她 _____ 要給她朋友打電話_____。

3. 小張的女兒要跟她爸爸去看一部很 _____ 的電影。

Follow-up Activities 應用

大家來說 Role-Playing (Oral)

Divide into groups of three and imagine the conversation that will take place after Xiao Zhang's wife returns. Each speaker should have at least five lines.

大家來寫 Role-Playing (Written)

Below is a movie schedule. Answer the questions based on the information in the ad.

What is the name of the film advertised?

_____

How many times will it play at the Méihuā 梅花 movie theater?

_____

If you wanted to see the film at 6:00 p.m., which theater would you go to?

What is the latest time you could see this film? Which theater would you go to?

_____

Which shows are discounted (hint: 特價 tèjià: special price)? How much do tickets for these shows cost?

_____

Where did this film have record-breaking sales?

❑ 台灣   ❑ 美國   ❑ 日本   ❑ 韓國

Which movie company produced this film?

❑ 中央電影公司   ❑ 天空之城

❑ 日本電影公司   ❑ 龍貓電影公司

Now you are ready to design your own ad for a film. Be sure to include the same type of information that was in the ad on the previous page. You could also add the name of the director, lead actors/actresses, or any other information you think would be of interest.

Preparation 熱身

What do you think is most important to do when studying a foreign language? Please rank the following activities in the spaces provided (1 = most important; 8 = least important).

Memorize new vocabulary   _____

Listen to audio recordings   _____

Watch videos or DVDs   _____

Study grammar   _____

Visit the country where the language is spoken   _____

Practice speaking   _____

Practice writing   _____

Use computer-based language learning programs   _____

▶ Listening for the Gist 泛聽

What is Xiao Zhang doing when he runs into Xiao Li?
- ❑ Studying in the library
- ❑ Grading papers
- ❑ Listening to audio tapes
- ❑ Running some errands

Why are they discussing dates and times?
- ❑ They are arranging when to have lunch.
- ❑ They are arranging when to take a class together.
- ❑ They are arranging when to go shopping.
- ❑ They are arranging when to go to the movies.

▶ Listening for Details 靜聽

Xiao Li thought Xiao Zhang was listening to. . .

❑ Japanese language tapes

❑ English language tapes

❑ music

On the calendar below, mark which days Xiao Zhang has Japanese lessons this month. Today is marked.

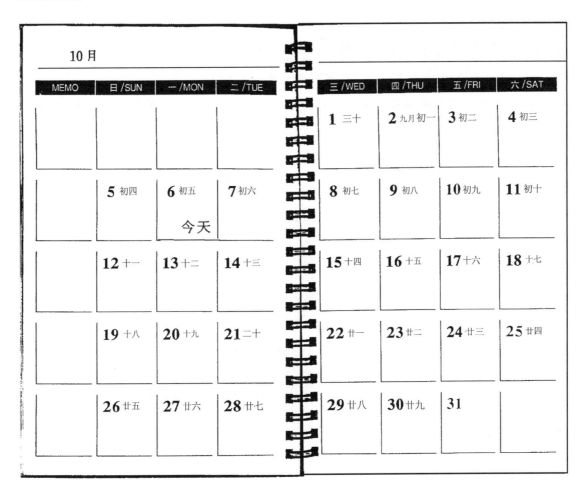

What time are his lessons?

❑ 2:00 p.m.

❑ 4:00 p.m.

❑ 2:30 p.m.

❑ 10:00 a.m.

❑ 5:00 p.m.

Why is Xiao Zhang studying Japanese?

❑ To do business

❑ To be able to read original works of Japanese literature

❑ To be able to talk to his Japanese classmates

❑ To help with his studies of Chinese literature

小李跟小張覺得學日文的時候最難的是

❑ 發音   ❑ 認識字   ❑ 語法   ❑ 説話

Key Language Points 語言點

Which of the following comments does Xiao Li make in this conversation? (circle all that apply)

A. 怎麼學都學不好   我一點都不忙

B. 怎麼學也學不好   我一點也不忙

What is the difference in meaning between sentence A and sentence B?

_____

_____

_____

Please answer the following questions using the pattern: 一點都(也)不.

1. 小李覺得學日文很容易嗎？

_____

2. 小張今天很累 (lèi: to be tired) 嗎？

_____

3. 小李喜不喜歡吃日本菜？

_____

4. 日文的語法小李都懂嗎？

_____

Follow-up Activities 應用

大家來説 **Role-Playing (Oral)**

_____

Xiao Zhang called his Japanese tutor that night to tell him about Xiao Li's interest in learning Japanese. "Recreate" this conversation with a partner. Be sure to explain Xiao Li's background and schedule. (The tutor's Chinese is perfect!)

大家來寫 **Role-Playing (Written)**

_____

Later Xiao Zhang and Xiao Li decided since their levels are different it would be better for them to take lessons separately. Xiao Li sent a note to the tutor explaining this situation and setting up an appointment for her first class. Please help her write this note. Be sure to include the place and times she can meet.

_____

_____

_____

_____

_____

_____

_____

Preparation 熱身

Identify the following actions using the appropriate Chinese characters:

_____ _____ _____

_____ _____ _____

聽廣播 tīng guǎngbō

看電視 kàn diànshì

看報直 kàn bàozhǐ

看照片 kàn zhàopiàn

照相　zhàoxiàng　　　　　(also 拍照[片] pāi zhào[piàn])

著急　zhāojí, zháojí　　　to be worried or concerned

Additional Useful Vocabulary

什麼的	shénme de	N	and the like, and so on, et cetera.
等等	děngděng	N	and the like, and so on, et cetera. [same as 什麼的]
興趣	xìngqù	N	interest/to be interested in: 對__有興趣/感兴趣
越來越	yuè lái yuè	Conj	more and more

Examples:

1. N 越來越 + V/Adj

小李越來越喜歡説英文。

Xiao Li likes speaking English more and more.

小李的功課越來越難。

Xiao Li's schoolwork is getting more and more difficult (or is getting harder).

2. V 得越來越 + V/Adj

她翻譯得越來越快。

She translates more and more quickly.

3. V + O + V + 得越來越 + V/Adj

小李説英文説得越來越好。

Xiao Li is speaking English better.

專業	zhuānyè	N	major/specialty
感覺	gǎnjué	N	feeling
根本	gēnběn	Adv	basically, fundamentally
進步	jìnbù	N	progress

What do you find most challenging about studying Chinese? (check all that apply)

❑ Remembering new words.
❑ Learning grammar.
❑ Writing characters.
❑ People have accents that are hard to understand.
❑ Learning traditional characters.
❑ Learning simplified characters.

How do you think learning Chinese compares to learning other languages and to learning English as a second language? List three specific examples of what is different about studying Chinese. Then list three things that are the same no matter what language is being studied.

Different	Same

▶ Listening for the Gist 泛聽

The main topic of this conversation is:

- ❏ Li Wenying's experiences studying English.
- ❏ Li Wenying's experiences teaching Chinese.
- ❏ Zhang Linsheng's experiences studying English.
- ❏ Zhang Linsheng's experiences teaching English.

Who do you think speaks English better? Why?

_____

_____

▶ Listening for Details 靜聽

How old was she when she first started studying English?

- ❏ 4 years old
- ❏ 6 years old
- ❏ 8 years old
- ❏ 10 years old
- ❏ 12 years old

Which of the following types of school does she mention?

- ❏ Elementary
- ❏ Middle school
- ❏ Graduate school
- ❏ High school
- ❏ College

Based on her comments, circle whether her teacher(s) at each level she mentioned was/were Chinese or American and indicate what she says about the emphasis of the classes she took.

Type of school	Type of teacher	Emphasis
Elementary	中國人 美國人	reading _____ speaking _____ writing _____ grammar _____
Middle school	中國人 美國人	reading _____ speaking _____ writing _____ grammar _____
High school	中國人 美國人	reading _____ speaking _____ writing _____ grammar _____
College	中國人 美國人	reading _____ speaking _____ writing _____ grammar _____

After coming to the United States, what does Xiao Li say she has done to improve her English? Check all that apply.

- ❏ Listened to the radio.
- ❏ Gone to the movies.
- ❏ Watched television.
- ❏ Made friends with Americans.
- ❏ Listened to language tapes.
- ❏ Exchanged language lessons with an American classmate.

What suggestion(s) does Xiao Li make to Xiao Zhang as a way he can improve his English? (check all that apply)

- ❏ She will introduce him to her American friends.
- ❏ He should watch more American TV.
- ❏ He should play soccer with her and her American friends.
- ❏ He should play basketball with her and her American friends.
- ❏ He should try to speak only English with his classmates.

Key Language Points 語言點

Here are two ways to say "I am interested in. . .":

我對 _____ 有興趣。

我對 _____ 感興趣。

Distinguish this from:

_____ (很)有意思。

Listen to the conversation again and indicate how many times these expressions are used and by whom.

	# of times spoken	spoken by Li	spoken by Zhang
我對 _____ 有興趣			
我對 _____ 感興趣			
_____ 很有意思			

Based on the following pictures, which expression would you use? In some cases you may be able to use both.

Example:

這個表演 (biǎoyǎn: performance) 很有意思。　她對運動有興趣。

_____　　　　　_____

越來越 V/Adj

Create one sentence using 越來越 based on the following information.

Example:

> 小張以前買的書很便宜。現在他買的書很貴。
>
> ↳　小張買的書越來越貴。

1. 小李去年不會跳舞。她現在跟幾個朋友學跳舞。

_____

2. 小張每天練習踢足球。他進步了很多。

_____

3. 小李住在中國的時候，覺得中國電影沒有意思。她來美國以後就很喜歡看中國電影了。

_____

Follow-up Activities 應用

大家來說 **Role-Playing (Oral)**

Xiao Zhang's wife has decided she really wants to learn English better. If you were Xiao Zhang, what kind of advice would you give her? Act out your speech with a partner.

大家來寫 **Role-Playing (Written)**

The next day Xiao Li introduced Xiao Zhang to one of her American friends who speaks Chinese. Here's what they said. Imagine you are Eric Davis and complete the dialogue. Make sure that you explain how long you've been studying Chinese. Ask Zhang how long he studied English, what he thinks is most challenging about studying foreign languages, etc.

李：我給你們介紹一下，這是我的同學張林生，這位是我的美國朋友，Eric Davis。

張：你好!

Davis: 你好。你來美國多久了?

张：已經五年多了。你學中文學了多久? 怎麼說得這麼好?

Davis: 哪裡哪裡，我 _____。

_____

_____

_____

_____

_____

Preparation 熱身

Useful Vocabulary

選	xuǎn	V	to choose
教書	jiāoshū	V	to teach
華僑	huáqiáo	N	overseas Chinese; foreign citizens of Chinese origin (also *華裔 huáyì)
上學	shàng xué	V	to go to school, to attend school
保重身體	bǎozhòng shēntǐ	VO	to take care of yourself, to pay attention to your health

*華裔 huáyì is a term used to refer to an American-born Chinese

Describe the make-up of your Chinese class. Be sure to include the number of teachers, students, women/men. Are any of your classmates 華僑?

_____

_____

_____

_____

_____

_____

_____

▶ Listening for the Gist 泛聽

What does Xiao Li say is her greatest difficulty in living in the U.S.?

- ❏ She is too lonely.
- ❏ She is too tired.
- ❏ She misses her daughter.
- ❏ She is too busy.
- ❏ She can't get used to the pace of life in the U.S.

Is Xiao Zhang sympathetic to her problem? How do you know?

_____

_____

Check all the topics that were mentioned in this conversation:

	✓
Li Wenying's graduate studies	
Li Wenying's teaching responsibilities	
Zhang Linsheng's teaching responsibilities	
How often Li Wenying gets together with her students	
What Li Wenying does to relax	

▶ Listening for Details 靜聽

How long has Xiao Li been in the U.S. when this conversation takes place?

- ❏ 3 months
- ❏ 9 months
- ❏ 6 months
- ❏ 1 year

How many classes is Xiao Li taking this semester?

- ❏ 1
- ❏ 3
- ❏ 2
- ❏ 4

What level Chinese class is Xiao Li teaching?

❏ First year   ❏ Second year

❏ Third year   ❏ Fourth year

Complete the following chart that describes the makeup of the students in her class.

Female students	
Male students	
Chinese-American students	
Total number of students	

除了教書以外，小李說她還做什麼？　(check all that apply)

❏ 在圖書館工作

❏ 在圖書館做研究

❏ 幫學生的忙

❏ 改 (gǎi: to correct) 作文

❏ 每天得上學

❏ 去書店買書

Key Language Points 語言點

Circle all the words in the following narrative that have to do with time.

小張來美國已經五年了。他剛來的時候一點也不習慣。除了要一邊上課一邊教書以外，那個時候他還要每天在圖書館工作。後來他慢慢習慣了。雖然現在得做的事情跟以前一樣多，可是小張覺得生活越來越有意思。他常常說，如果我不這麼忙，就會覺得生活太無聊。

Now translate this narrative into English.

_____

_____

_____

_____

_____

_____

_____

In this conversation Xiao Zhang says "一年級挺不好教的." What does he mean?

❑ It's really not easy to teach first-year Chinese.

❑ It's really not good to teach first-year Chinese.

❑ He really doesn't like to teach first-year Chinese.

❑ Students in first-year Chinese aren't really very good.

Follow-up Activities 應用

大家來說 Role-Playing (Oral): Interview

Interview two students and complete the chart:

	第一個學生	第二個學生
名字		
幾年級的學生		
專業		
選幾門課		
選什麼課		
上課的時間		
有沒有工作		
工作的地方		
工作的時間		

Here is a list of Xiao Li's activities for tomorrow. Help her arrange a schedule. Please write it out in Chinese characters on the next page.

She teaches Chinese (10:00–11:00 a.m.).

She helps students with pronunciation (1:00–2:00 p.m.).

She eats breakfast at 7:00 a.m., lunch at 11:30 a.m., and dinner at 6:45 p.m.

She has a seminar on Chinese literature (3:30–5:50 p.m.).

She needs to prepare for her seminar on Chinese linguistics which meets the following day.

She needs to grade students' homework assignments.

She has to go to the library to check out a book.

She needs to call her husband in China (remember the time difference).

She has to buy a bus pass.

Preparation 熱身

Identify the following items using the appropriate Chinese characters:

_____ _____ _____ _____

_____ _____ _____ _____

_____ _____ _____ _____

外套 wàitào	帽子 màozi	雨傘 yǔsǎn	帶子 dàizi
襯衫 chènshān	襪子 wàzi	裙子 qúnzi	褲子 kùzi
毛衣 máoyī	鞋子 xiézi	西裝 xīzhuāng	領帶 lǐngdài

Additional Useful Vocabulary

服裝	fúzhuāng	N	clothing etc. (男裝／女裝)
挑	tiāo	V	to select, pick
肯定	kěndìng	Adv	definitely

▶ Listening for the Gist 泛聽

How did Xiao Zhang and Xiao Li get together at the store?

- ❏ They arranged to meet there.
- ❏ They just happened to run into each other.
- ❏ They took the bus there together after class.

Which of them has already made purchases?

- ❏ 李文英   ❏ 张林生

What do they decide to do at the end of their conversation?

- ❏ Continue shopping
- ❏ Get something to eat
- ❏ Get something to drink
- ❏ Go home

▶ Listening for Details 靜聽

Which of the items listed above has Xiao Li purchased? Check all that apply.

- ❏ 外套   ❏ 毛衣
- ❏ 帽子   ❏ 鞋子
- ❏ 襪子   ❏ 裙子

Which item's color does she mention?

❑ 外套   ❑ 毛衣

❑ 帽子   ❑ 鞋子

❑ 襪子   ❑ 裙子

Which items does Xiao Zhang say he wants to buy?

❑ 外套   ❑ 毛衣

❑ 帽子   ❑ 鞋子

❑ 襪子   ❑ 領帶

❑ 西裝

What is Xiao Li's favorite color?

❑ 藍色   ❑ 紅色

❑ 黃色   ❑ 紫色

❑ 綠色   ❑ 灰色

What did Xiao Li buy for her daughter?

❑ 毛衣   ❑ 外套

❑ 鞋子   ❑ 裙子

❑ 襪子   ❑ 帽子

What size shoes does Xiao Zhang wear?

❑ 8

❑ 8 ½

❑ 9

❑ 9 ½

❑ 10

Key Language Points 語言點

Choose the proper measure word for each of these items from the list given below. Keep in mind that some items can have more than one correct measure word.

位　條　門　件　個　把　部　本　隻

雙　杯　枝　封　瓶　節　套　間　張　頂

_____ 外套	_____ 帽子	_____ 鉛筆	_____ 茶
_____ 雨傘	_____ 衣服	_____ 襯衫	_____ 襪子
_____ 裙子	_____ 褲子	_____ 毛衣	_____ 鞋子
_____ 西裝	_____ 領帶	_____ 字典	_____ 信
_____ 筷子	_____ 桌子	_____ 電影	_____ 課
_____ 汽水	_____ 椅子	_____ 老師	_____ 朋友

NOTE: The second time Li Wenying mentions what she bought for her daughter, she uses the generic measure word gè 個 instead of tiáo 條 or jiàn 件. Sometimes people inadvertently forget to use the more appropriate measure word and just use 個 instead. Be careful not to fall into this habit!

Degrees of Certainty

Since Xiao Li is certain that the store sells the kind of shoes Xiao Zhang wishes to buy, she says 肯定有 ("they definitely have them").

Compare the range of certainty expressed by the following adverbial expressions:

肯定(一定)　　　　definitely

大概　　　　　　　probably

也許 (yěxǔ), 可能　　possibly

不可能　　　　　　impossible

絕對 (juéduì) 沒/不　absolutely impossible, definitely doesn't

Now answer the following questions indicating an appropriate degree of certainty.

1. 小張買得到十塊錢的鞋子嗎？

_____

2. 小李想不想她女兒？

_____

3. 如果小張也給他女兒買一件裙子，她會很高興嗎？

_____

4. 小張可不可以穿九號的鞋子？

_____

5. 飯館賣不賣服裝？

_____

6. 外套比毛衣貴嗎？

_____

7. 服裝商店賣不賣褲子跟領帶？

_____

8. 下雨的時候你會帶雨傘嗎？

_____

Follow-up Activities 應用

大家來説 Role-Playing (Oral)

Xiao Li and Xiao Zhang went to the men's section of the store where Xiao Zhang is considering purchasing a sweater, a pair of shoes, and a jacket. Xiao Li also remembered she needs to buy an umbrella. Enact a conversation in which they help each other select from the following items.

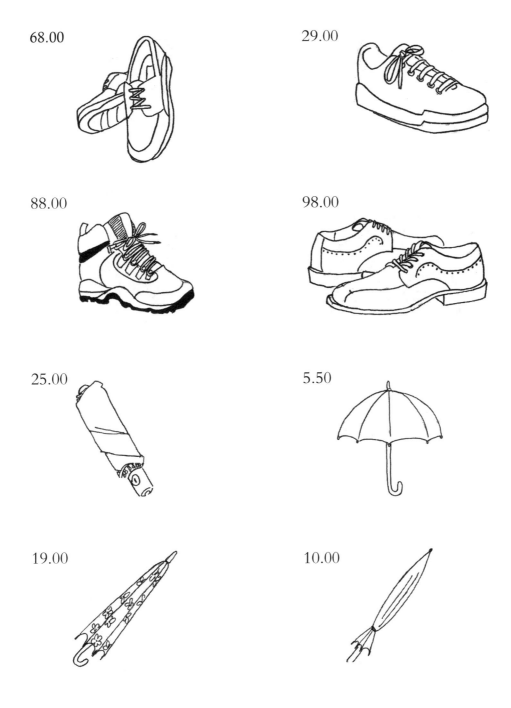

68.00

29.00

88.00

98.00

25.00

5.50

19.00

10.00

59.00
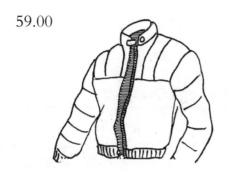

19.50

45.00

45.00
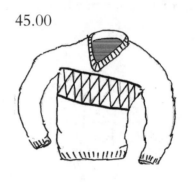

28.00

179.00

大家來寫 Role-Playing (Written)

Answer the questions based on the receipts given below.

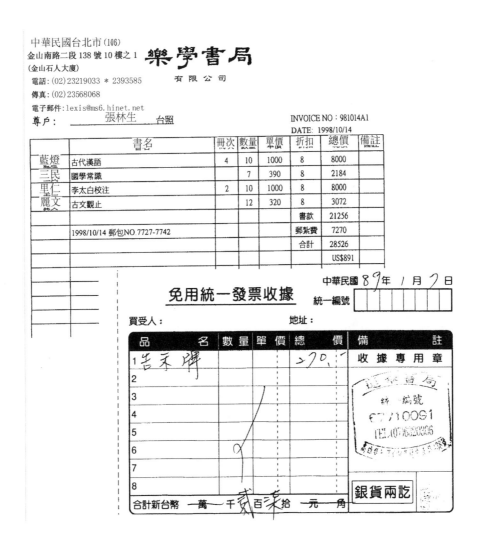

1. When were the purchases made?

_____

2. How many books were purchased?

_____

3. What was the exchange rate used in the receipt from 樂學書局?

_____

4. What is the fax number for 樂學書局?

_____

5. Who is the publisher of the book 國學常識?

_____

6. Which store gave a discount and how much of a discount was given?

_____

7. What do you think the characters 貳 and 柒 mean in the second receipt?

_____

_____

Preparation 熱身

Write the appropriate season 季節 (jìjié) shown in these pictures.

_____   _____

_____   _____

冬天 dōngtiān   夏天 xiàtiān   春天 chūntiān   秋天 qiūtiān

How many of these words can you use to describe the people and situations in the following pictures?

熱 rè　　　　　晴 qíng　　　　陰 yīn　　　　冷 lěng　　　　刮風 guā fēng

涼快 liángkuài　　　下雨 xiàyǔ　　　多雲 duōyún　　　潮濕 cháoshī

乾燥 gānzào　　　舒服 shūfu　　　下雪 xià xuě　　　悶 mēn

_____ _____

_____ _____

_____ _____

_____ _____

Additional Useful Vocabulary

遲到	chídào	V	to be late
走過來/走過去	zǒuguòlái/zǒuguòqù	V	walk towards/walk away

Here are two examples of how these expressions are used idiomatically.

1. Why does the speaker apologize in the first example?

2. Where is the speaker in the second example located? How do you know?

因為我早上很晚才起床，所以上課<u>遲到了</u>。<u>真對不起</u>。

如果你現在有時間，就<u>走過來</u>。<u>你家離我家很近</u>。

▶ Listening for the Gist 泛聽

Of the following topics, indicate which ones you heard mentioned in the dialogue:

	✓
Why Xiao Zhang arrived late	
When Xiao Zhang arrived	
Making an apology	
The location at which they met	
The reason for them getting together	
The weather that day	
The weather yesterday	
The forecast for tomorrow	
The weather in Beijing	
The season with the best weather in Beijing	
The coldest month in Beijing	
The season the wind blows the most	

▶ Listening for Details 靜聽

Complete the following sentences according to what you heard in the dialogue. Put a check by the correct answer.

Xiao Zhang was late because he. . .

	✓
lost track of time	
missed the bus	
couldn't start his car	
was shoveling snow	

How did Xiao Zhang get to school? He. . .

	✓
drove	
walked	
took the bus	

What does Xiao Li say about the weather today compared with yesterday?

❑ Windy but warmer　　　❑ Very windy and snowy

❑ Windy and colder　　　❑ Warmer and sunnier

❑ Not as much snow but very windy

Fill out the chart describing the weather in Beijing based on what Xiao Zhang says.

	hot	cold	humid	dry	stuffy	windy	snowy	rainy	cool
winter									
spring									
summer									
fall									

In what season does he consider the weather in Beijing to be ideal?

	✓
winter	
spring	
summer	
fall	

Key Language Points 語言點

Distinguish between these two expressions:

1. 從來不 + verb   2. 從來沒 verb 過

Example:

我從來不吃肉。

我從來沒吃過日本菜。

I never eat meat. (habitual action)

I have never eaten Japanese food. (past experience)

Listen to the conversation again. Which expression does Xiao Zhang use? How many times does he use it?

_____

_____

Answer the following questions using either 從來不 or 從來沒. Be careful—some questions can be answered with either expression but the meanings will be different.

1. 你去過內蒙古 (Nèi Měnggǔ: Inner Mongolia) 嗎?

_____

2. 你的朋友天天喝咖啡嗎?

_____

3. 你每個週末都打排球嗎?

_____

4. 你的同學喜不喜歡看中國電影?

_____

Idiomatic expression:

What do you think Xiao Zhang means when he says, "北京不怎麼下雪"?

❑ It doesn't snow that much in Beijing.

❑ It doesn't snow this much in Beijing.

❑ It's impossible for it to snow in Beijing.

❑ It's unlikely it will ever snow in Beijing.

Compare the pictures in Column B with Column A, using the pattern B 比 A + Adj.
(example: 夏天比春天悶).

| Column A | Column B |

Follow-up Activities 應用

大家來説 **Role-Playing (Oral)**

With a partner: Compare the weather in the different seasons based on the picture. Discuss what the weather is like where you live now compared to the weather in the hometown where you grew up.

On the following page is a weather report. Where do you think it was published? Why?

台北市	多雲短暫雨	19~23°C	廣州	多雲	17~26°C
基隆北海岸地區	陰有雨	19~23°C	福州	多雲	16~22°C
台北地區	多雲短暫雨	18~23°C	重慶	陰	13~17°C
桃竹苗地區	多雲局部短暫雨	18~25°C	漢口	晴	10~20°C
台中彰化地區	多雲局部短暫雨	18~27°C	杭州	晴	10~19°C
南投地區	多雲短暫雨	18~27°C	上海	晴	12~19°C
雲林嘉義地區	多雲短暫雨	17~27°C	南京	晴	9~19°C
台南高雄地區	多雲短暫雨	20~28°C	北平	多雲	6~15°C
屏東地區	多雲短暫雨	21~29°C	開封	多雲	6~12°C
恆春半島	陰時多雲有雨	22~28°C	西安	多雲	6~12°C
宜蘭地區	陰有雨	18~22°C	洛陽	多雲	4~10°C
花蓮地區	陰時多雲有雨	20~26°C	香港	多雲	20~26°C
台東地區	陰時多雲有雨	21~28°C	東京	晴	13~21°C
澎湖地區	多雲短暫雨	21~25°C	漢城	晴	6~15°C
金門地區	多雲時晴	18~25°C	曼谷	雨	25~30°C
馬祖地區	多雲時晴	15~20°C	新加坡	雨	24~31°C
			巴黎	晴	8~12°C
			倫敦	晴	4~11°C
			紐約	陰	6~9°C
			洛杉磯	陰	17~25°C
			舊金山	陰	16~20°C
			多倫多	晴	0~7°C
			約翰尼斯堡	晴	9~26°C

今日天氣

Describe the weather in the following places (hint: 短暫 duǎnzàn: short duration, brief):

Tainan:

_____

Nanjing:

_____

Hong Kong (香港 Xiānggǎng):

_____

Paris (巴黎 Bālí):

_____

大家來寫 **Role-Playing (Written)**

That night Xiao Zhang called a Chinese friend of his who lives in California and told him about the unusual weather. Write down how you think this conversation went. Each speaker should have at least eight lines.

_____

_____

_____

_____

_____

_____

_____

_____

_____

Preparation 熱身

Identify the following pictures using the appropriate Chinese characters from the next page:

_____

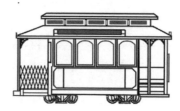

_____

_____

_____

公路   電車   自行車/脚踏車   (zìxíngchē/jiǎotàchē)

高速公路   汽車   出租汽車/計程車   (chūzūqìchē/jìchéngchē)

公共汽車   飛機   摩托車   (mótuóchē)

地鐵(地下鐵路)   行李   火車   (huǒchē)

Useful Vocabulary

機場	jīchǎng	N	airport, also 飛機場
寒假	hánjià	N	winter break
春假	chūnjià	N	spring break
暑假	shǔjià	N	summer break
接/送	jiē/sòng	V	to meet/ to see off
麻煩	máfán	N	trouble, troublesome, bother, bothersome
危險	wēixiǎn	Adj	dangerous (also pronounced wéixiǎn)
辦法	bànfǎ	N	method, way, means
方法	fāngfǎ	N	method, way, means
恐怕	kǒngpà	V	I'm afraid that ..., I'm worried that ...
		Adv	perhaps, possibly
提前	tíqián	Adv	in advance

How far is the airport from where you live? What is the best way to get there? How long does it take to drive there? How much does it cost to go by taxi? By bus? What are some advantages and disadvantages of each means of transportation?

	advantages	disadvantages
private car		
taxi		
bus		
other		

▶ Listening for the Gist 泛聽

What did Li Wenying ask Zhang Linsheng? (check all that apply)

	✓
Driving directions to get to the airport	
Alternatives to driving to the airport	
If he will drive her to the airport	
How long it takes to drive to the airport	
If he has ever driven to the airport	
If roads are dangerous in the snow	

Why is she going to the airport?

❑　She is picking up her parents.

❑　She is going on a trip.

❑　She is picking up a friend.

❑　She is picking up her husband and daughter.

▶ Listening for Details 靜聽

When does Xiao Li need to go to the airport?

❑　The next day　　　　❑　During spring break

❑　During winter break　　❑　During summer break

Which highways does Xiao Zhang mention? (check all that apply)

❑　36　　❑　76　　❑　270　　❑　287

❑　25　　❑　79　　❑　70　　❑　225

What advantages and disadvantages do Xiao Zhang and Xiao Li mention concerning each of these transportation options?

	advantages	disadvantages
driving		
taxi		
bus		

Where is the bus station located?

❑ 15th St.

❑ 16th St.

❑ 45th St.

❑ 5th St.

Key Language Points 語言點

恐怕

Answer the following questions or respond to the situations described using 恐怕.

Example:

今天天氣會怎麼樣?

↳　恐怕今天會下雨。

1. 小李要去機場接她的朋友,可是她不要開車。

_____

2. 小李的朋友行李多不多?

_____

3. 下雪的時候開車危險嗎?

_____

When Xiao Zhang learns that Xiao Li just learned how to drive he says,

"要是這樣的話,你最好不要開車。"

("If that is the case, it would be best for you not to drive.")

要是…(的話) or 如果…(的話) means "if."

Rewrite the following sentences using 要是…的話 (or 如果…的話).

Example:

下雪的時候小李不開車。

↳ 要是下雪的話，小李會坐公共汽車。

1. 坐火車比坐飛機便宜多了。

_____

2. 高速公路上，車都開得很快。

_____

3. 小李不知道公共汽車站在哪兒。

_____

Follow-up Activities 應用

大家來說 Role-Playing (Oral)

With a partner: Ask about the last time you went to the airport. Why were you there? How did you get there? What is your favorite/ least favorite airport? Why?

大家來寫 Role-Playing (Written)

This is the first time Xiao Li's friend has left China. She plans to stay for 4½ weeks. Besides visiting Xiao Li, she would like to go to Disneyland and also visit classmates who live in New York City 紐約, San Francisco 舊金山, and Chicago 芝加哥. Here is the itinerary the travel agent came up with; can you help complete it?

洛杉磯　Luòshānjī　　　Los Angeles

紐約　Niǔyuē

舊金山　Jiùjīnshān

芝加哥　Zhījiāgē

日期	班次	目的地	登機時間	座號
12/16	UA 1146	洛杉磯	8:36am	22A

Preparation 熱身

Chinese food is usually divided into four styles of cooking: Northern, Eastern, Western, and Southern. The regions that are associated with these styles can be seen on this map.

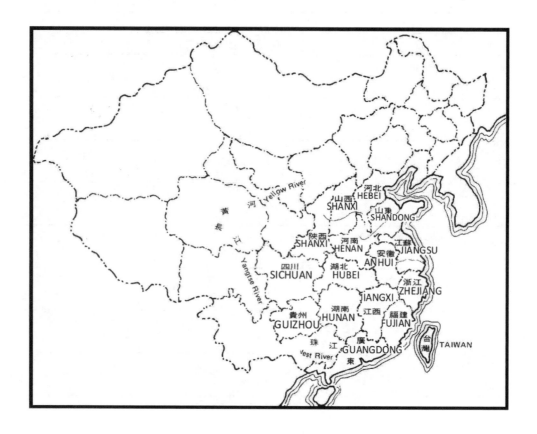

北方菜	東方菜	西方菜	南方菜
河北	江蘇	四川	廣東
山西	浙江	湖南	福建
河南	安徽	貴州	台灣
山東	湖北		
陝西	江西		

Wheat is a staple in Northern cooking: noodles, steamed bread and steamed buns, and ravioli-like dumplings (steamed, boiled, or fried) are frequently served. Rice is the staple in Southern cooking: steamed or fried rice, rice noodles, or sticky rice generally accompany dishes from this area. Chinese cooking emphasizes flavor, color, aroma, and presentation. Here are the main flavors in Chinese cuisine.

辣	là	hot, spicy
甜	tián	sweet
鹹	xián	salty
酸	suān	sour
苦	kǔ	bitter

Additional Useful Vocabulary

春節	chūnjié	N	Spring Festival (Chinese New Year)
熟悉	shúxī	V	知道得很清楚
風味	fēngwèi	N	flavor
清淡	qīngdàn	Adj	light (of food)
比如	bǐrú	Adv	for example
吃素	chīsù	VO	to be a vegetarian
比較	bǐjiào	Adv	relatively, comparatively (also pronounced bǐjiǎo)
像	xiàng	Adv	such as (像…等[等]: such as, …etc.) In formal writing 等 is used instead of 等等.

Examples: See if you can translate these sentences into English in the spaces provided.

小李看過很多國家 (guójiā: country) 的電影，像美國的，日本的，法國的，還有英國的。

小張吃過很多種 (zhǒng: kinds, types) 中國菜，像北京菜，上海菜，四川菜，廣東菜，等等。

_____

_____

_____

要不	yàobu	Conj	short for 要不然 yàobùrán: otherwise
師傅	shīfu	N	master (chef)
味道	wèidào	N	flavor, taste, smell, odor
油	yóu	N/Adj	oil, oily (also cunning, slippery when describing a person)
膩	nì	Adj	greasy; bored, tired of

Example: See if you can translate this sentence into English.

我天天聽那位大師傅的故事，已經聽膩了。

_____

_____

What are your favorite Chinese foods? Do you know what regional style of cooking these dishes are?

_____

_____

_____

_____

_____

▶ Listening for the Gist 泛聽

The main topic of this conversation is. . .

- ❑ finding places for vegetarians to eat
- ❑ comparing different styles of Chinese cooking
- ❑ choosing a Chinese restaurant
- ❑ Chinese restaurants where Li Wenying's students like to eat

Which of the following dishes are mentioned?

			✓
糖醋魚	tángcù yú	Sweet and Sour Fish	
家常豆腐	jiācháng dòufǔ	Family-style Tofu	
清蒸魚	qīngzhēng yú	Steamed Whole Fish	
宮爆雞(丁)	gōngbào jī (dīng)	Gongbao Chicken	
麻婆豆腐	mápó dòufǔ	Mapo Tofu	
紅燒牛肉	hóngshāo niúròu	Braised Beef	
涼拌菜	liángbàn cài	Chinese-style Shredded Salad	
冬菇菜心	dōnggū càixīn	Black Mushrooms & Chinese Cabbage	
魚香茄子	yúxiāng qiézi	Eggplant with Hot Garlic Sauce	

Who has a friend who is a chef? (circle one)

李文英　　　張林生

▶ Listening for Details 靜聽

Xiao Li wants to take her students out to eat because. . .

- ❑ the semester is almost over.
- ❑ it's almost Chinese New Year.
- ❑ it's almost spring break.
- ❑ it's almost the end of the school year.

Complete the chart below based on the information given in the conversation:

	東方樓	金龍
region of cuisine		
dominant flavor		
suggested dishes		
recommended for vegetarians?		

Which restaurant does she decide to go to? (circle one)

東方樓   金龍

Why?

_____

_____

_____

When will the dinner be held?
- ❑ Thursday
- ❑ Friday
- ❑ Saturday
- ❑ Sunday

What is the chef's last name? (circle one)

王   毛   高   鄭

劉   周   孔   梁

What decision is made at the end of the conversation?
- ❑ Xiao Zhang will order for them.
- ❑ Xiao Zhang will talk to the owner.
- ❑ Xiao Zhang will talk to the chef.
- ❑ Xiao Zhang will join the class for dinner.

Key Language Points 語言點

Listen to the conversation again and fill in the blanks below with the verbs that are used with these objects.

_____菜　　_____學生　　_____時間　　_____吃辣　　_____大師傅

熟／對…熟 (悉 xí)／跟…熟

shú／shóu*　　1. to be familiar with

2. to be ripe, to be well cooked, mature

*NOTE: Generally speakers from Taiwan say shóu for both meanings and prefer not to use 熟悉. When 熟悉 is used as a compound, it is pronounced shúxī.

See if you can translate these sentences into English. Notice how 熟 means something different in each case.

1. 水果不熟的話就不好吃。

_____

2. 這種菜煮熟了才有味道。

_____

3. 他是我小學同學，我們兩個非常熟。

_____

4. 小張對這個城市的中國飯館很熟悉。

_____

5. 那條路小李常常走，所以她很熟。

_____

每⋯都⋯ měi...dōu...

Do you remember in this conversation when Li Wenying says "每個菜都很辣"? How would you translate her comment?

_____

_____

Rewrite the following sentences using the pattern 每⋯都⋯, then translate each sentence into English.

Example:

這個飯館的菜很辣。

↳   這個飯館的每個菜都很辣。

Every dish at that restaurant is spicy.

1. 我星期一到星期天吃米飯。

_____

2. 我們家對面有五個美國大學生住在一起。沒有一個人會做菜。

_____

3. 中國留學生過年的時候會想家。 (liúxuéshēng: foreign student)

_____

4. 師傅希望客人吃得很高興。

_____

5. 吃素的美國人願意吃中國菜嗎？ (yuànyì: to be willing to)

_____

Follow-up Activities 應用

大家來說 **Role-Playing (Oral)**

With a partner, plan a dinner for twelve people (some of whom are vegetarians) at a Chinese restaurant in your area. First compare two or three Chinese restaurants. Be sure to discuss the type of Chinese cuisine they offer, the price, location, and whether they would be able to accommodate a large party. Now design the menu, naming the specific dishes you will order.

Reading

When some of Li Wenying's students went to China recently they realized that they didn't know how to determine the kind of restaurant by the sign. One hint they discovered was that often the formal name for the region that indicated the style of cooking was given (instead of the informal name). Here are some examples:

Formal name	Informal name
魯 Lǔ	山東 Shāndōng
湘 Xiāng	湖南 Húnán
粵 Yuè	廣東 Guǎngdōng
閩 Mǐn	福建 Fújiàn
豫 Yù	河南 Hénán
蜀 Shǔ	四川 Sìchuān
滬 Hù	上海 Shànghǎi

Sometimes restaurants simply used the abbreviated form of the region. What do you think are the full names of the places indicated by these single characters?

川   Chuān   _____

京   Jīng   _____

港   Gǎng   _____

津   Jīn   _____

台   Tái   _____

Here are some restaurant names and phone numbers taken from a Beijing public phone book.

東方滬園大酒樓	6833 0321
東方江湘菜美食城	6524 3040
五湘齋飯莊	6512 0076
東北骨頭飯館	6842 1848
甘肅餐廳	6605 7398
世界層脊青稞酒家	6401 8822-1852 (西藏)
北京人新粵他酒樓	6801 0681
北京珠江漁村酒樓	6126 8409
醉紅潮州城	6303 6530
川好味重慶菜	6326 9682
巴蜀風大酒樓	6764 7296
魯味餐廳	6201 5165
魯豫餐廳	6815 7739
川魯園餐廳	6437 3182
居德林菜館	6404 5967 (素菜)

Answer the following questions based on these names.

1. Give the name and telephone number of the restaurant that specializes in these types of cuisine:

a. Cantonese _____

b. Shanghainese _____

d. Tibetan (Xīzàng) _____

c. Hunanese _____

2. How many restaurants offer Sichuan-style cooking?

_____

3. Which restaurant might be most appealing to a vegetarian?

_____

4. If someone wanted to eat authentic Shandong jiǎozi, which restaurant(s) might they try?

_____

Preparation 熱身

Useful Vocabulary

你幹嘛呢	Nǐ gànmá ne?	Coll	What are you up to/What are you doing?
讀	dú	V	to read
半天	bàntiān	N	half a day; a long time
書架	shūjià	N	book shelf
查	chá	V	to look up information; to investigate
查字典	chá zìdiǎn	V	to look something up in a dictionary
電腦	diànnǎo	N	computer
情況	qíngkuàng	N	situation, circumstances; 情形
實際上	shíjìshàng	Conj	as a matter of fact (cf. shìshíshàng 事實上, qíshí 其實, actually)
亂	luàn	Adj	disorganized, chaotic
短	duǎn	Adj	short, 不長
書名	shū míng	N	一本書的名字
怎麼辦	zěnme bàn	Coll	What can be done?
沒事(兒)	méishèr	Coll	"You're welcome." (PRC)

How often do you go to the library? What are some of the problems you have encountered? How have you resolved them? What do you think would be the best way to improve library services on your school campus or in your community?

_____

_____

_____

_____

_____

▶ **Listening for the Gist** 泛聽

What is Zhang Linsheng's general mood in this conversation? Why do you think this is?

_____

_____

Check the topics that Xiao Zhang and Xiao Li mention in this conversation.

- ❏ Li Wenying's search for one particular book
- ❏ How to use the computer to search for books
- ❏ Why Zhang Linsheng doesn't like to go to the library
- ❏ Hours that the library is open
- ❏ Problems with overdue fines
- ❏ How books are checked out in libraries in China
- ❏ A library project Xiao Li is working on with her classmates

▶ **Listening for Details** 靜聽

What is the title of the book is Xiao Li looking for?

- ❏ 中國文選史
- ❏ 中國文學史
- ❏ 中國文選
- ❏ 中國語言學史

In looking for this book, which of the following actions has Xiao Li done?

- ❏ Checked the shelves
- ❏ Checked the computer database
- ❏ Asked the librarian
- ❏ Checked inter-library loan
- ❏ Checked the cart with books to be shelved
- ❏ Checked to see if any of her classmates own this book
- ❏ Checked to see if any of her classmates have checked out this book

Which of the above options does Xiao Zhang suggest that Xiao Li do?

_____

_____

Which three things does Xiao Zhang mention that are different between this library and the one he used in China?

- ❏ In China there are no open stacks.
- ❏ The librarians are more helpful in China.
- ❏ The librarians are more helpful in the U.S.
- ❏ Libraries are open for longer hours in China.
- ❏ Libraries are open for longer hours in the U.S.
- ❏ There are more computers in libraries in the U.S.
- ❏ Libraries in China are quieter than those in the U.S.
- ❏ Libraries in the U.S. are quieter than those in China.
- ❏ Library fines in the U.S. are more expensive that those in China.

Key Language Points 語言點

Fill in the blanks based on what was said in the conversation. Choose from the following words or phrases (hint: not all these words were used, and the words may be used more than once).

誰	圖書館	要是	借	同學	好
然後	拿	特別	把	雖然	幫

1. 你＿＿＿＿書名寫＿＿＿＿給圖書館員。他會＿＿＿＿你＿＿＿＿書
　　找到。

2. ＿＿＿＿書的時間＿＿＿＿很長，但是＿＿＿＿過期，罰金＿＿＿＿貴。

3. 找咱們的＿＿＿＿看看他們＿＿＿＿有這本書，＿＿＿＿向他＿＿＿＿
　　一下。

Now translate each of the completed sentences into English.

1. ＿＿＿＿＿＿＿＿＿＿＿＿＿＿＿＿＿＿＿＿＿＿＿＿＿＿＿＿＿＿＿

　＿＿＿＿＿＿＿＿＿＿＿＿＿＿＿＿＿＿＿＿＿＿＿＿＿＿＿＿＿＿＿

2. ＿＿＿＿＿＿＿＿＿＿＿＿＿＿＿＿＿＿＿＿＿＿＿＿＿＿＿＿＿＿＿

　＿＿＿＿＿＿＿＿＿＿＿＿＿＿＿＿＿＿＿＿＿＿＿＿＿＿＿＿＿＿＿

3. ＿＿＿＿＿＿＿＿＿＿＿＿＿＿＿＿＿＿＿＿＿＿＿＿＿＿＿＿＿＿＿

　＿＿＿＿＿＿＿＿＿＿＿＿＿＿＿＿＿＿＿＿＿＿＿＿＿＿＿＿＿＿＿

How would you translate the phrase 我找了半天也沒有找到?

＿＿＿＿＿＿＿＿＿＿＿＿＿＿＿＿＿＿＿＿＿＿＿＿＿＿＿＿＿＿＿＿

＿＿＿＿＿＿＿＿＿＿＿＿＿＿＿＿＿＿＿＿＿＿＿＿＿＿＿＿＿＿＿＿

Follow-up Activities 應用

大家來說 Role-Playing (Oral)

That morning Lin Wenying spoke with a classmate she saw in the library and he said he'd help her track down the book she needs. That evening he called her and they talked about this issue and some of their concerns regarding the library. With a partner, enact this conversation.

大家來寫 **Role-Playing (Reading)**

Based on the library card on the following page, give the following information:

Name of library _____

Gender of card holder _____

When the card expires _____

Which of the following is NOT mentioned on the back of the card?

❑ Hours that the library is open

❑ Whether the card can be used at other libraries

❑ Whether the card can be used for other purposes

❑ What you should do when the card expires

❑ What happens if you lend the card to someone else to use

❑ What you should do if the card gets ripped or is lost

❑ What someone who finds the card should do

What year does 民國77年 correspond to?

❑ 1977

❑ 1987

❑ 1988

Do you know why?

_____

_____

_____

國立圖書館
閱 覽 證

閱覽證號	4 203 7X71	性別	F

姓　名	李文英

有效日期	民國 77 年 12 月 31 日

發證日期	民國 76 年 1 月 23 日

備　註	☑核發　□補發　□換發

注 意 事 項

1. 憑本證，填寫閱覽記錄單後，於管制口，入繳交，出領回。

2. 應遵守本館一切閱覽規則。

3. 本證如自行塗改變換或缺少照片印章或轉借他人，均視爲無效並沒收之。

4. 本證遺失或破損不堪使用時應即按照手續向本館申請補換，未辦補換手續而重領新證者，一經查出即予沒收。

5. 本證專供在本館之用，不得作爲其他證明，否則一經查出，印子作廢。

Preparation 熱身

Identify the following items using the appropriate Chinese characters.

_____

_____

_____

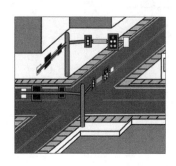

_____

_____

_____

十字路口　shízìlùkǒu
紅綠燈　hónglǜdēng
購物中心　gòuwù zhōngxīn

招牌　zhāopái
電影院　diànyǐngyuàn
馬路　mǎlù

Additional Useful Vocabulary

老板(闆)	lǎobǎn	N	owner, boss
經常	jīngcháng	Adv	常常
校園	xiàoyuán	N	campus
向…拐	xiàng…guǎi	Prep	turn in x direction at … (向左/右拐)
	or zhuǎn 轉	V	turn left, turn right at … (used in northern dialects)
之後	zhī hòu	Suf	以後 (cf. 之前, 之間, 等等)
不多久	bùduōjiǔ		before very long
歡迎(你)	huānyíng (nǐ)	Ph	(generally occurs as 歡迎光臨)
光臨	guānglín		↳ "We welcome your patronage" (frequently said to customers when entering or leaving a store).

▶ Listening for the Gist 泛聽

Who recommended that Li Wenying call this place?

_____

_____

Why did Li Wenying make this call?

_____

_____

▶ Listening for Details 靜聽

Whom did Xiao Li speak with?

- ❑ 陳老板 Chén
- ❑ 沈老板 Shěn
- ❑ 鄭老板 Zhèng
- ❑ 程老板 Chéng
- ❑ 趙老板 Zhào

Based on the directions he gave, draw a map showing how to get to the restaurant from school.

Where is the restaurant located? (check all that apply)

- ❑ Between the movie theater and shopping center
- ❑ In the shopping center
- ❑ Next to the shopping center
- ❑ Across the street from the shopping center
- ❑ Across from the movie theater
- ❑ Near the movie theater

When did Xiao Li say she would come to the restaurant?

_____

_____

_____

Key Language Points 語言點

用 and 把

Before giving directions, the man on the phone said 你用筆記一下. Distinguish the difference between 用 and 把.

Fill in the blanks of the sentences below with either 用 or 把 and then translate each sentence into English.

1. 李文英每天_____筷子吃飯。

_____

2. 因爲小李不在家，所以她_____她朋友的電話給陳老板打電話。

_____

3. 小李_____筆畫一張地圖。

_____

4. 她畫完以後，_____地圖給她的學生。

_____

5. 小李的學生_____地圖找金龍飯店。

_____

6. 陳老板_____菜單給金龍飯店的大師傅。

_____

7. 劉師傅_____很新鮮 (xīnxiān: fresh) 的材料 (cáiliào: ingredients) 做菜。

_____

8. 菜做好了以後，小姐_____菜放在桌子上。

_____

9. 小李跟她的學生_____現金 (cash) 付帳 (fùzhàng: pay restaurant bill)。

_____

10. 陳老板_____收據 (shōujù: receipt) 給小李。

_____

11. 李文英的學生_____中文給陳老板寫信。

_____

12. 陳老板_____這封信貼 (tiē: to stick on) 在飯館的牆 (qiáng: wall) 上。

_____

＊　＊　＊

Here are some directions you might give to a friend who is driving or to a cab driver. See if you can translate them into Chinese.

1. Turn left at the shopping center.

_____

2. Turn right after the bookstore.

_____

after = yǐhòu
before = yǐqián

3. Stop at the third intersection after the movie theater.

_____

4. The Chinese restaurant I'm looking for is across from campus.

_____

✳   ✳   ✳

不多久

The man on the phone says, "你不多久會看到我們的飯店." Which sentence(s) is/are closest in conveying the sense of this sentence? (check all that apply)

❑ 你很快就可以看到我們的飯店。

❑ 你等一下會看到我們的飯店。

❑ 你要等很久才會看到我們的飯店。

❑ 你馬上就看到我們的飯店。

Follow-up Activities 應用

大家來說 Role-Playing (Oral)

One of Xiao Li's students mistakenly left a backpack at the restaurant and had to call Chen Laoban to see if it was there. In enacting this phone conversation, be certain to tell him what color the bag is and what was inside. You will also need to identify yourself, and it might also be nice to thank him for the trouble he went to in arranging the class dinner.

大家來寫 Role-Playing (Written)

Xiao Li's students enjoyed the meal so much that they decided it would be fun to write a note to the owner of the restaurant thanking him for his help and telling him how great the food was. On the next page, write what you think this letter might say.

Just for fun

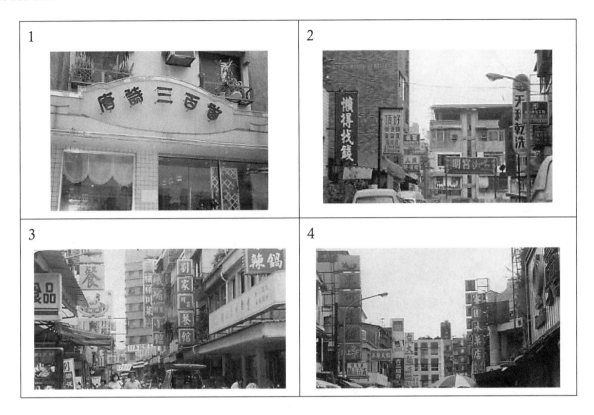

Below are some translations of signs from restaurants in Taipei. See if you can find the sign that is translated. Write the number of the photo in which each 招牌 appears.

	#
Too Lazy to Give Change	
300 Poems of the Tang Dynasty	
Mike's Steaks	
Taiwan University Noodle Shop	
The Liu Family Sichuan Style Restaurant	
The Honey Garden Ices and Fruit Shop	

Preparation 熱身

Identify the following items using the appropriate Chinese characters

_____ _____ _____

_____ _____ _____

蛋糕 dàngāo　　　小朋友 "little friends," general term for one or more kids

禮物 lǐwù　　　麵 (or miàntiáo 麵條)　　老人　　商場 shāngchǎng

Additional Useful Vocabulary

訂	dìng	V	to order
講究	jiāngjiù	Adj	particular about, meticulous, exacting

What do you usually do when you plan a birthday party or when you are invited to attend one? List three things.

_____

_____

_____

What do you think might be some differences between the ways birthdays are celebrated in the United States and in China? List two things. (You might want to look back at your notes from Lesson 3.)

_____

_____

_____

Based on this chart of the Chinese zodiac signs, answer the questions that follow it.

鼠	shǔ	rat		1948; 1960; 1972; 1984; 1996; 2008
牛	niú	ox, cow		1949; 1961; 1973; 1985; 1997; 2009
虎	hǔ	tiger		1950; 1962; 1974; 1986; 1998; 2010

兔	tù	rabbit, hare		1951; 1963; 1975; 1987; 1999; 2011
龍	lóng	dragon		1952; 1964; 1976; 1988; 2000; 2012
蛇	shé	snake, serpent		1953; 1965; 1977; 1989; 2001; 2013
馬	mǎ	horse		1954; 1966; 1978; 1990; 2002; 2014
羊	yáng	sheep, goat		1955; 1967; 1979; 1991; 2003; 2015
猴	hóu	monkey		1956; 1968; 1980; 1992; 2004; 2016
雞	jī	rooster, chicken		1957; 1969; 1981; 1993, 2005; 2017
狗	gǒu	dog		1958; 1970; 1982; 1994; 2006; 2018
豬	zhū	pig, boar		1959; 1971; 1983; 1995; 2007; 2019

你屬什麼? _____

如果小李屬馬, 小張屬牛, 他們兩個大概幾歲?

小李: _____歲

小張: _____歲

▶ Listening for the Gist 泛聽

Check the topics that Xiao Zhang and Xiao Li mention in this conversation.

❏ Whose birthday it is

❏ Age of this person

❏ When and where the birthday party will take place

❏ How many people will attend the party

❏ What activities are planned for the party

❏ What kinds of food will be served

❏ Differences between American and Chinese ways of celebrating birthdays

❏ Other birthday parties they have been to recently

Where is Zhang Linsheng headed when this conversation takes place?

❏ To the market

❏ To school

❏ Returning home

What does Li Wenying offer to do to help celebrate this birthday?

_____

_____

▶ Listening for Details 靜聽

See if you can answer the following questions using pīnyīn or Chinese characters.

Who is having a birthday?

_____

How old is this person?

_____

In what year do you think s/he was born? (You may want to refer to the chart given on the preceding pages.)

_____

Why is Xiao Li surprised to hear that Xiao Zhang is giving a birthday party?

_____

Whose birthday did Xiao Li celebrate when she went to China last year?

_____

How was that birthday celebrated?

_____

How many people were invited?

_____

Why does Xiao Zhang say "你太客氣了"?

_____

Check the correct responses based on the conversation.

How many children are invited to the party?

    ❑ More than 10   ❑ 16

    ❑ Fewer than 10   ❑ 10

    ❑ Around 10

小李要給小張的女兒什麼?

    ❑ 毛衣   ❑ 裙子

    ❑ 鞋子   ❑ 帽子

    ❑ 褲子

Key Language Points 語言點

訂/定

訂 dìng means to:

reserve   subscribe to   order   make an agreement

Example:

Xiao Zhang says he's going to 訂一個蛋糕...

定 dìng means to:

determine   set   decide on   make definite

Example:

When Xiao Li goes shopping for a birthday present, the shop owner 已經定了價錢.

NOTE: Sometimes the meanings overlap and these distinctions are not strictly followed.

How would you translate 訂/定 when it takes the following nouns as objects?

_____ 飯館	_____ 婚	_____ 一件外套
_____ 規矩	_____ 義	_____ 火車票
_____ 合同	_____ 貨	_____ 報紙
_____ 牛奶	_____ 日期	_____ 主意
_____ 時間	_____ 雜誌	_____ 座位

How would you translate Zhang Linsheng's comment "美國人很講究過生日"?

_____

_____

The expression 講究 is often used to describe people who are particularly concerned with the precise way things are done, e.g., 穿衣服, 寫字, 吃東西, 喝茶, 等等. List three more situations (in Chinese) in which someone could be considered 講究 or 不講究.

_____   _____   _____

* * *

A few days later Zhang Linsheng explained to his American friend some of the differences between the ways that Americans and Chinese celebrate birthdays. Complete the following paragraph using these words:

讓	得	所以	高興	不一樣	的	碗
最多	很少	請客	過	講究	只有	

在美國過生日跟在中國過生日_____。美國人比較_____過生日。在中國_____給孩子過生日，_____吃一_____麵條就是了。在中國，_____老人才_____生日。過生日_____人一定要吃麵。因為麵條很長，_____有長壽 (chángshòu: long life) 的意思，_____過生日的人覺得很_____。

Now translate this paragraph into idiomatic English.

_____

_____

_____

_____

_____

Follow-up Activities 應用

大家來說 Role-Playing (Oral)

Later that day Li Wenying ran into Xiao Zhang's wife and they talked about the upcoming birthday party. Act out this conversation with a partner. Be sure to use these words or phrases: 過生日, 訂蛋糕, 屬, 送禮物, 吃麵條, 講究.

Last week Xiao Zhang's neighbor had a birthday party for her daughter. Here are some pictures of the party. On the next page, write two sentences describing each picture.

Preparation 熱身

Identify the following pictures using the appropriate Chinese characters from the next page.

_____

_____

_____

_____

_____

_____

_____

_____

_____

瘦	shòu	冷氣	lěngqì	藥	yào
發燒	fāshāo	咳嗽	késòu	打針	dǎzhēn
醫院	yīyuàn	住院	zhùyuàn	躺	tǎng

Additional Useful Vocabulary

好幾天	hǎo jǐ tiān		many days
一下子	yíxiàzi	Adv	all at once
開心	kāi xīn	Adj	高興
特別	tèbié	Adv	especially
嚴重	yǎnzhòng	Adj	serious
拖	tuō	V	to delay, to procrastinate

Unfortunately people sometimes get sick when they are traveling. List some reasons why this might occur. Have you ever had this kind of experience? If so, describe what happened.

_____

_____

_____

_____

_____

_____

_____

Since the opposite of 外 is 內 (nèi), what do you think 國內 and 國外 mean?

_____

In the conversation you will hear in this lesson, 國內 refers to _____ and 國外 refers to _____.

倒 dào, on the contrary, shows the opposite of what was expected.

Examples:

妹妹十歲，姐姐十四歲，妹妹倒比姐姐高。

Younger sister is 10 and older sister 14, but (much to our surprise) younger sister is taller than older sister.

她住得最近，倒來得最晚。

She lives the closest but it turns out that she arrived latest.

How would you translate this sentence?

沒看醫生，她的病倒好了。

_____

_____

* * *

一會兒A，一會兒B

One minute this, one minute that.

Example: How would you translate this sentence?

他一會兒要看電影，一會兒要去跳舞，就是不要在家裡看書。

_____

_____

反正   fǎnzhèng   anyway, in any case

Examples: How would you translate these sentences?

我可以送你回家，反正我家離你家很近。

_____

_____

他買不買還不一定，反正我要買。

_____

_____

▶ Listening for the Gist 泛聽

Where did Xiao Li just return from?

❑ Changchun   ❑ Nanjing

❑ Beijing   ❑ Shanghai

Was she sick in China or did she fall ill after she returned?

_____

Check all the topics Xiao Li and Xiao Zhang mentioned in this conversation.

	✓
Her symptoms when she first didn't feel well	
Taking over-the-counter cold medicine	
Drinking herbal tea	
Staying in bed all day	
Going to the hospital	
Getting shots	
Her family's concern for her health	

▶ Listening for Details 靜聽

What were Li Wenying's symptoms?

❑ Fever   ❑ Muscle soreness

❑ Diarrhea   ❑ Sneezing

❑ Cough   ❑ Fatigue

❑ Headache

How long was she in the hospital?

❑ 2 days   ❑ 3 days

❑ 4 days   ❑ A week

Based on this experience, what does she resolve to do in the future? (check all that apply)

❑ 不能拖   ❑ 要把冷氣關掉

❑ 要多吃感冒藥   ❑ 一發燒就要躺下來

❑ 一生病就得去看醫生   ❑ 要多注意身體

Key Language Points 語言點

Listen carefully to the beginning of the conversation, paying special attention to these lines:

張：怎麼你一下子瘦了那麼多啊！我看你是不是在國內玩得太累了？

李：那倒不是，在國內玩得挺開心，但是就是我病了一個多星期。

Translate into English what Xiao Zhang said, paying special attention to the uses of 得.

_____

_____

_____

Explain the function of the 倒 in Xiao Li's response.

_____

_____

Go back and underline the descriptive complements (or resultative clauses) introduced by 得.

Complete the following sentences. Remember that what comes after 得 shows a comment on or the result of the verb.

1. 小李病得_____。

2. 小李的丈夫著急得_____。

3. 那個星期小李藥吃得_____。

4. 醫院的醫生忙得_____。

5. 過了一個星期小李就累得_____。

In this conversation Xiao Li said that she 不能不去醫院. How would you translate her statement?

_____

_____

Chinese frequently uses double negatives. Circle the negatives in the following paragraph. Then translate the paragraph into idiomatic English.

小李剛回家的時候沒覺得不舒服。可是過了幾天，她就又咳嗽又發燒了。丈夫勸 (quàn: to advise) 小李去看病，可是到了醫院以後才發現那兒的醫生沒有一個不忙。小李知道她這麼不舒服，非等不

可 (i.e., 不能不等)。過了一個半小時，醫生才給她看病，告訴小李感冒的時候不能不在家休息。再說，她不可以不吃藥。醫生還提醒 (tíxǐng: to remind) 她，一個人不能不注意自己的身體，沒有人不願意健康 (jiànkāng: healthy)。小李心裡想，她如果不聽醫生的話，就好不了 (hǎobuliǎo: won't get better) 了。她家裡的人也都同意，而且很高興小李沒得 (dé: to get) 什麼治不了 (zhìbuliǎo cannot be cured) 的病。

Follow-up Activities 應用

大家來說 Role-Playing (Oral)

With a partner, imagine the conversation that took place when Li Wenying went to the hospital in China. It turned out that the doctor she saw was a friend of her parents, and in fact this doctor's son was also studying in graduate school in the U.S. So they had a lot to talk about in addition to Li Wenying's health problems. Be sure to include the following vocabulary: 不舒服, 特別, 其實, 躺, 反正, 怪不得, 嚴重, 拖, 好幾天, 身體, 健康, verb +得+ descriptive complement.

Reading

A few weeks later Xiao Li's uncle fell ill. On the following page is a prescription he was given. Complete this chart based on the information in the prescription.

Patient's name	
Age	
Patient's medical history number	
Date prescription was written	
Name of hospital that filled the prescription	
How high should patient's temperature be before he takes aspirin?*	
How often should he take aspirin?	
How often should he take the second medicine that is prescribed?	
Doctor's family name	

*NOTE: Remember, it's given in Celsius, not Fahrenheit.

宏恩醫院
處 方 箋

病歷號 71489

住院號 _____

姓名 王天竟 年齡 48 性別 男   處方號 _____

R   2008 年 6 月 21 日

1, 阿司匹靈 0.3 X 12

　　服法：佳溫超過攝氏三十八度
　　　　　時每四至六小時服一粒

2, 紅徽素 0.5 X 12

　　服法：每六小時服一丸

醫師 李睿辰 配方藥師 _____ 校正藥師 _____

Preparation 熱身

Useful Vocabulary

單獨	dāndú	Adj/Adv	alone, individually, on one's own
週年	zhōunián	N	anniversary
説來就長	shuōlái jiù cháng	Coll	it's a long story (also 説來話長)
編輯	biānjí	N	editor
夫婦	fūfù	N	couple, husband and wife
丈夫	zhàngfu	N	husband (also 先生)
慶祝	qìngzhù	V	to celebrate
左右	zuǒyòu	Suf	approximately
單位	dānwèi	N	unit (in an organization or administration)

▶ Listening for the Gist 泛聽

Why did Zhang Linsheng call Li Wenying?

- ❑ He wants her to babysit.
- ❑ He wants her to join him and his wife for dinner and a movie.
- ❑ He wants advice about buying an anniversary present for his wife.
- ❑ He wants to invite her over tomorrow night for dinner.

How long have Zhang Linsheng and his wife been married?

- ❑ 8 years
- ❑ 12 years
- ❑ 10 years
- ❑ 11 years

How did they first meet?

_____

_____

▶ Listening for Details 靜聽

What day of the week is it?

❑ Thursday   ❑ Saturday

❑ Friday   ❑ Sunday

What kind of jobs did Zhang Linsheng and his wife have when they first met?

_____

_____

_____

What prompted them to start dating?

_____

_____

How long did they date before they got married?

❑ Six months   ❑ Two years

❑ One year   ❑ Three years

What time does Xiao Zhang want Xiao Li to come to their house?

❑ 5:30   ❑ 6:30

❑ 6:00   ❑ 7:00

What time do they plan to return?

❑ 10:00   ❑ 11:00

❑ 10:30   ❑ 12:00

Key Language Points 語言點

Write the pīnyīn for the measure words or classifiers (量詞 liàngcí) Xiao Zhang uses for these nouns.

_____電影   _____飯

What 量詞 should be used with these objects?

封   張   棵 kē   輛 liàng   條

把   座 zuò   朵 duǒ   付   所

_____   _____   _____

_____   _____   _____

_____   _____   _____

In Chinese some words, known as 破音字 pòyīnzì or 多音字 duōyīnzì, have more than one pronunciation, depending on the meaning. For example, kàn usually means to read, but when it's pronounced in the first tone it means to look after, to watch (remember Xiao Zhang asks Xiao Li to 看孩子 kān háizi).

Here are some other common words that are sometimes pronounced in different tones. The pinyin for each pronunciation and examples of compounds with each pronunciation are given in this chart. Complete the chart. The first entry has been done for you.

Character	Pīnyīn	Compounds	Pīnyīn	English
假	jiǎ	假如	jiǎrú	if
	jià	放假		
好	hǎo	很好		
	hào	愛好		
教	jiāo	教書		
	jiào	佛教	fójiào	
樂	lè	快樂		
	yuè	音樂		
長	cháng	長城	chángchéng	
	zhǎng	長大		
少	shǎo	多少		
	shào	少年		young adults, juvenile
得	dé	跑得快		
	děi	得上課		
大	dà	長大		
	dài	大夫	dàifu	
分	fēn	一分錢，分開		
	fèn	身分		
重	zhòng	重要		
	chóng	重寫		

Character	Pīnyīn	Compounds	Pīnyīn	English
差	chā	差不多		
	chà	差		
	chāi	出差		to go on a business trip
種	zhǒng	各種		
	zhòng	種菜		
論	lùn	討論	tǎolùn	
	lún	論語		
覺	jué	覺得		
	jiào	睡覺		
要	yào	要是		
	yào	重要		
	yào	要面子		
	yāo	要求	yāoqiú	
看	kàn	看法		
	kān	看家		

Complete these sentences using the appropriate pòyīnzì/duōyīnzì chosen from the preceding table. Write the Chinese characters and pīnyīn. Then translate each sentence into English.

1. 張林生和他太太還沒結婚的時候，常常聽＿＿＿＿＿＿＿＿。因爲這是他們的＿＿＿＿＿＿＿。

2. ＿＿＿＿＿＿＿＿李文英要六點鐘＿＿＿＿＿＿＿張林生的女兒，她＿＿＿＿＿＿＿五點四十＿＿＿＿＿＿＿離開她的家。

3. 小李到張家的時候，張太太正在＿＿＿＿＿＿＿菜。她女兒在她房間＿＿＿＿＿＿＿。

4. 小張的女兒喜歡留 (liú: to [let] grow)＿＿＿＿＿＿頭髮 (tóufa, tóufǎ: hair) 可是她媽媽＿＿＿＿＿＿這樣不好＿＿＿＿＿＿。

5. 小李的學生對印度 (Yìndu: India) 很有興趣。他們的＿＿＿＿＿＿＿請了一個老師＿＿＿＿＿＿＿佛＿＿＿＿＿＿＿(Buddhism) 的課。他們非常＿＿＿＿＿＿＿。

6. 小李也告訴她的學生＿＿＿＿＿＿＿是一本很＿＿＿＿＿＿＿的書。＿＿＿＿＿＿＿每個中國學生都知道這本書。

Follow-up Activities 應用

大家來説 Role-Playing (Oral)

The way that Xiao Zhang and his wife dated before they got married is fairly typical for many Chinese students. What are some ways that their experience differs from dating practices in the U.S.? With a partner discuss the strengths and weaknesses of each system. Be sure to use some of these words and expressions:

同學　對象　朋友　一起　左右　認識　出去　跳舞　週末

大家來寫 Role-Playing (Written)

Create a dialogue in Chinese based on the picture on the next page. First provide some background information, such as the names of the people who speak, where and when the conversation takes place, and a sentence saying how well they know each other.

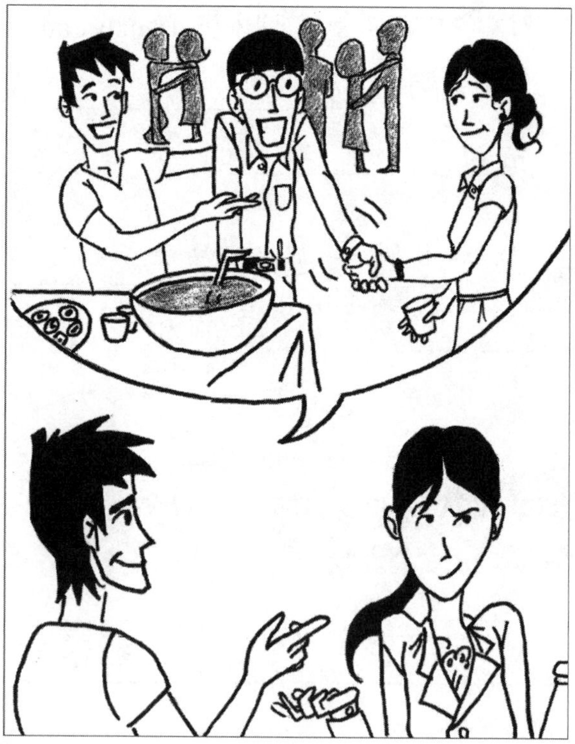

Lesson 18 第十八課
Renting an Apartment 租房子

Preparation 熱身

Useful Vocabulary

簽證	qiānzhèng	N	visa
換	huàn	V	to change
合適	héshì	Adj	suitable
搬家	bānjiā	V	to move
包括	bāokuò	V	to include

If you were looking for an apartment (gōngyù 公寓), what would matter most to you? Rank in order of importance, one (1) being highest.

_____ location 地點

_____ deposit 押金 (yājīn)

_____ size of living room 客廳

_____ number of units in building

_____ number of bathrooms 洗澡間

_____ number of bedrooms 臥室

_____ cost of rent 房租

_____ cost of utilities 水電費

_____ term of contract 租約期限 (zūyuē qíxiàn or qīxiàn)

_____ type of landlord 房東

_____ availability of parking 車位

_____ convenience of public transportation 交通

▶ Listening for the Gist 泛聽

Why is Li Wenying looking for an apartment?

_____

_____

How does Zhang Linsheng think he can help her?

_____

_____

▶ Listening for Details 靜聽

What does Xiao Li mention regarding her apartment hunting? (check all that apply)

❑ location   ❑ number of bedrooms

❑ amenities   ❑ cost of rent

❑ deposit   ❑ cost of utilities

❑ size of living room   ❑ term of contract

❑ number of units in building   ❑ type of landlord

❑ number of bathrooms   ❑ availability of parking

Complete the chart based on the information Zhang Linsheng gives about his friend.

name	
telephone number	
location of apartment	
size of apartment	
cost of rent	
cost of utilities	
when the apt will be available	

When does Xiao Li say she will call Xiao Zhang's friend?

❑ Right away   ❑ Tomorrow morning

❑ This afternoon   ❑ Tonight

❑ After she talks to her husband

Key Language Points 語言點

Verb + 得/不 + 下 Potential Complements

Toward the beginning of this conversation Xiao Li makes the following comment: 以前我住在一個一個臥室的公寓裡. 他們來了就住不下了. How would you translate her statement? (Hint: 住不下 means "won't be able to live there any longer.")

_____

_____

Complete these sentences using one of the following verbs plus either 得下 or 不下, depending on the context. Some verbs may be used more than once.

吃　　喝　　住　　坐　　放

1. 那個電影院很小，恐怕_____一百多人。

2. 雖然他們家很小，可是書架很多，張林生剛買的書一定_____ _____。

3. 我們一邊聊天一邊喝茶，已經喝了兩三個小時，我真_____ _____了。

4. 這個教室非常大，兩百個人也_____。

5. 小李現在住的公寓不太大，她先生跟女兒來了以後，三個人就_____。

6. 小張上個星期六做了很多菜，像紅燒牛肉、麻婆豆腐、宮爆雞丁等等，最後還有一條很大的清蒸魚。他的太太跟女兒都＿＿＿＿＿＿了。

*　*　*

連…都（也）…

Xiao Zhang says that the apartment he knows about has this advantage: 連水電都包括. How would you translate his comment?

＿＿＿＿＿＿＿＿＿＿＿＿＿＿＿＿＿＿＿＿

＿＿＿＿＿＿＿＿＿＿＿＿＿＿＿＿＿＿＿＿

Based on the information in each of the following sentences, write a sentence using 連…都(也)…

Example:

本來小李的先生去年想來美國，可是她沒申請 (shēnqǐng: to apply for) 簽證。

↳   小李的先生去年連簽證都沒有申請。

1. 小李上個月天天找房子。下雪的時候她還去看了。

＿＿＿＿＿＿＿＿＿＿＿＿＿＿＿＿＿＿＿＿

2. 小李也打了很多電話。

＿＿＿＿＿＿＿＿＿＿＿＿＿＿＿＿＿＿＿＿

3. 小李覺得找房子很累。她沒時間吃飯。

＿＿＿＿＿＿＿＿＿＿＿＿＿＿＿＿＿＿＿＿

4. 這幾天天氣特別冷，小李又沒穿毛衣，也沒戴帽子，怪不得她感
冒了。

_____

5. 小李感冒的時候完全不願意吃藥。

_____

Follow-up Activities 應用

Xiao Li called Zhang Linsheng's friend to find out more about the apartment. Before she called she made a list of some additional things she wanted to ask about. In addition to things from the list above, she also wanted to ask if there's a playground or park nearby, what type of people live in the building, whether the building is noisy or if there is a lot of street noise, how close the apartment is to pre-schools or daycare centers. Write this list in Chinese.

_____   _____

_____   _____

_____   _____

大家來說 Role-Playing (Oral)

Now enact the above conversation with a partner.

大家來寫 Role-Playing (Written)

Here is an ad from a Chinese newspaper. Answer questions based on this ad.

Where do you think this newspaper is published? Why?

_____

What is the telephone number of the apartment for rent on Linsen 林森 North Rd.?

_____

Find the ad for the apartment on Da'an Rd. 大安路. What does it say about transportation?

_____

Circle the rental properties that advertise furnished apartments.

_____

Which property is close to the airport? Which property is near the train station?

_____

_____

Which ads are for business office space?

_____

_____

Preparation 熱身

Useful Vocabulary

Identify the following items using the appropriate Chinese characters:

  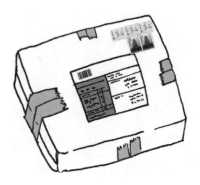

 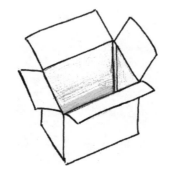 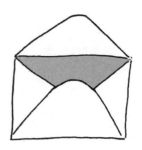

明信片　míngxìnpiàn 　　郵件　yóujiàn

郵票　　yóupiào 　　　　盒子　hézi

包裹　　bāoguǒ 　　　　信封　xìnfēng

Verbs 動詞

寄	jì	to send
郵	yóu	to mail
裝	zhuāng	to pack
運	yùn	to transport (海運 hǎiyùn, 空運 kōngyùn)
省	shěng	to save (省錢, 省事 to save trouble, to simplify matters)
收	shōu	to receive
貼	tiē	to affix, to paste

▶ Listening for the Gist 泛聽

What was Zhang Linsheng doing at the post office?

_____

What was Li Wenying doing at the post office?

_____

▶ Listening for Details 靜聽

Why does Xiao Li say "恭喜恭喜"?

❏ It's New Year's.

❏ Zhang Linsheng is about to graduate.

❏ Zhang Linsheng got a job in the U.S.

❏ Zhang Linsheng got a job in China.

Which of the following items does Zhang Linsheng say he is mailing?

❏ Books   ❏ Radio

❏ Clothes   ❏ Television

❏ Toys   ❏ Computer

❏ CD player

How long does Zhang Linsheng think it will take to mail packages by sea mail to China?

❑　Three weeks　　❑　Two months

❑　One month　　❑　Three months

❑　Two months　　❑　Four months

Based on the conversation, circle whether the following statements about Lin Wenying are true (是) or false (非).

她不知道張林生快要畢業了。	是	非
她看到了一個裝玩具的盒子。	是	非
她要買郵票。	是	非
她要寄包裹。	是	非
她要買明信片。	是	非
她要把明信片寄到中國。	是	非
她要把明信片寄到美國。	是	非
她要給她母親寫信。	是	非
她現在不忙，可以幫小張的忙。	是	非
她現在很忙，沒時間幫小張的忙。	是	非

Key Language Points 語言點

How would you translate:

國際 guójì　　　國內 guónèi　　　國外 guówài

In this dialogue, which countries are referred to as 國內 and 國外?

國內 = _____

國外 = _____

Modification with 的

Below are some phrases with 的. Write a complete sentence with each phrase, then translate the entire sentence.

Example:

装玩具的盒子

↳   張文生要把裝玩具的盒子寄到中國。

Zhang Wensheng is going to mail the box packed with toys to China.

1. 寄回去的衣服

_____

_____

2. 在美國買的電腦

_____

_____

3. 冬天戴的帽子

_____

_____

4. 在中國找到的工作

_____

_____

5. 貼在信封上的郵票

_____

_____

6. 在郵局見面的同學

_____

_____

7. 郵海運的英文書跟中文書

_____

_____

8. 前年在購物中心買的電視

_____

_____

9. 寄給朋友的明信片

_____

_____

10. 寄給住在國內的朋友的明信片

_____

_____

至少　　(zhìshǎo: at least)

Answer the questions using 至少.

Example:

寄海運慢不慢？

↳　很慢，至少要等三個月才到。

1. 小張要寄幾個盒子？

_____

2. 小李要買幾張郵票？

_____

3. 小張的太太衣服多不多？

_____

4. 那天郵局的人多不多？

_____

5. 你認為把電腦寄到中國貴不貴？

_____

Follow-up Activities 應用

大家來說 Role-Playing (Oral)

After waiting in line for 15 minutes, Zhang Linsheng is assisted by a postal worker who helps him decide the best way to mail his packages. He has to tell the worker what is in each box and whether he wants to send it air mail or sea mail. He asks when the boxes will probably arrive and how much it will cost to buy additional insurance. The postal worker tells him the cost of each package and asks him if he wants a receipt. Enact this conversation with a partner. The postal worker's first question is given below:

這個盒子裡裝的是什麼？

_____

_____

_____

_____

_____

_____

_____

大家來寫 **Role-Playing (Written)**

Meanwhile Li Wenying is at another counter buying stamps. Complete the conversation she is having with this postal worker:

李： 請問，你們這兒賣郵票嗎？

營業員： _____。你要買什麼樣的_____？

李： _____。

營業員： 這些明信片你要寄到哪兒？

李： _____。

營業員： 你有幾封信要寄？

李： _____。

營業員： 要寄到哪兒？

李： _____。

營業員： 寄到_____每張要_____錢，你要幾張？

李： _____。

營業員： 那一共要_____塊錢。你要不要一個收據？

李： _____。

營業員： 好，給你了。

李： 謝謝。

營業員： _____。

Reading

Below is a communication from the post office. What is the point of this notice?

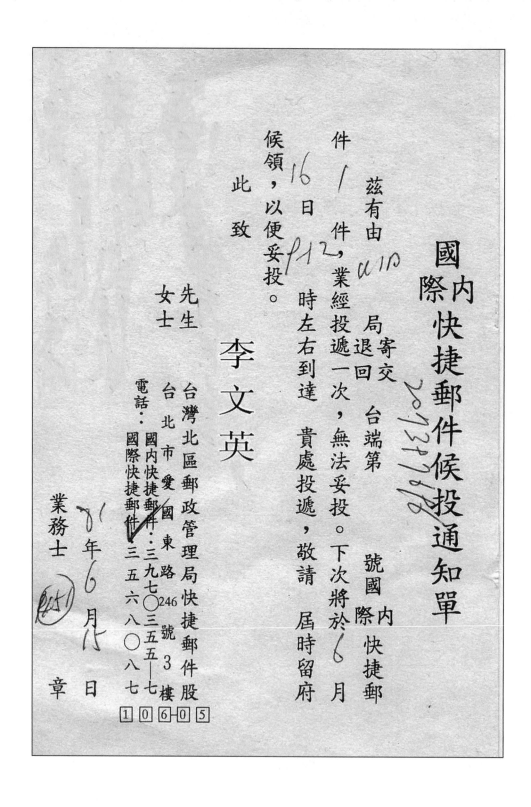

國內
國際快捷郵件候投通知單

茲有由　　　　　局寄交　台端第　　　　　號國內

件　　件，業經投遞一次，無法妥投。下次將於6月

16日　　時左右到達　貴處投遞，敬請　屆時留府

候領，以便妥投。

此致

　先生
　女士

李文英

台灣北區郵政管理局快捷郵件股
台北市愛國東路246號3樓
電話：
國內快捷郵件：三九七〇三五五七
國際快捷郵件：三五六八〇八七
106 05

業務士　　　　章

91年6月15日

1. When was the notice written?

_____

2. When will the post office attempt delivery again?

_____

3. How many items of mail are to be delivered?

_____

4. Is the mail international or national?

_____

5. Translate the complete address of the post office into English.

_____

_____

6. What number should one call for further information about this delivery?

_____

Preparation 熱身

Identify these sports using the appropriate Chinese characters:

_____ _____ _____

_____ _____ _____

_____ _____ _____

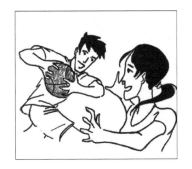

————————   ————————   ————————

踢足球	滑雪　huáxuě	溜冰　liūbīng
打乒乓球	打棒球　dǎ bàngqiú	打籃球
打網球	練太極拳　liàn taìjíquán	游泳
跑步	練劍術　liàn jiànshù	橄欖球　gǎnlǎnqiú＝美式足球

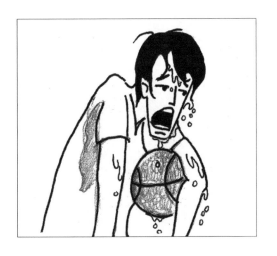

滿頭大汗

How would you translate this expression?

_____

▶ Listening for the Gist 泛聽

What is the main sport mentioned?

❑ football   ❑ basketball

❑ soccer   ❑ running

Who plays this/these sport(s)?

	played this sport in the past	plays this sport in the present
張林生		
李文英		
張林生和李文英		

▶ Listening for Details 靜聽

Who does Xiao Zhang play this sport with?

- ❑ Only Chinese men
- ❑ Mostly Chinese men and women
- ❑ Only American men
- ❑ Mostly American men and women

What is Xiao Li worried will happen if she plays this sport?

- ❑ She will be hurt.
- ❑ She will be embarrassed.
- ❑ She will not be as good as other players.
- ❑ She will be the only female player.
- ❑ Other players will laugh at her.

What does Xiao Zhang say to reassure Xiao Li that she is welcome to join him and his teammates? (check all that apply)

- ❑ 沒事了!
- ❑ 沒關係!
- ❑ 沒問題啊!
- ❑ 我們歡迎你參加!
- ❑ 不會的!
- ❑ 不要擔心啊!

How often does Xiao Zhang play this sport?

_____

When did Xiao Li play this sport?

❑ In middle school

❑ In high school

❑ In college

❑ After she graduated from college

Key Language Points 語言點

A. Arrange the sentences in the order they are spoken in the dialogue and circle who the speaker is.

_____我們星期六的下午三點開始踢。　　　小張　小李

_____那到時候我們一起去吧!　　　小張　小李

_____一般踢一個半小時。　　　小張　小李

_____剛跑步啊!　　　小張　小李

_____我已經有三年沒踢足球了。　　　小張　小李

_____我們一個星期一定要踢一次足球。　　　小張　小李

B. Go back and circle all the time words or expressions in these sentences. Note whether they indicate duration of time, approximate time or precise time.

C. Now translate each sentence, making sure you use the appropriate verb tense based on the information about time that is given.

_____

_____

_____

_____

_____

_____

_____

_____

*　*　*

這麼... 還...

Toward the beginning of the conversation Xiao Li says,

"這麼熱的天氣還踢足球?"

How would you translate this sentence? (Hint: there is more than one correct answer.)

❑　Even though it is so hot you still play soccer!

❑　How can you play soccer in such hot weather?

❑　How hot was the weather when you played soccer?

❑　Even you play soccer in such hot weather?

❑　Will you still play soccer if the weather is this hot?

❑　Why would anyone play soccer in such hot weather?

Translate each sentence into Chinese using 這麼…還… (Hint: Xiao Li could also have said 天氣這麼熱還踢足球 and it would have meant the same thing.)

1. Even though those tennis shoes are so expensive Xiao Li still wants to buy them.

_____

2. Xiao Li's roommate even goes jogging when there is so much traffic.

_____

3. The swimming pool is so far away but many students still swim there every day.

_____

4. Xiao Zhang's American friend plays basketball outside even in such cold weather.

_____

5. Taijiquan is so complicated (fùzá 複雜) yet a lot of people practice it often.

_____

6. Even though there are so few people, they still want to play baseball.

_____

Follow-up Activities 應用

大家來說 Role-Playing (Oral)

Recently Li Wenying's friend sent her some pictures of a taiqi class she is taking in China. With a partner describe what you see.

大家來寫 Role-Playing (Written)

Write a paragraph about a sport or activity you enjoy. Be sure to tell when you. . .

    played a sport for a specific amount of time.

    just recently played a sport.

    played a sport a certain number of times per week or month.

    played a sport at an exactly specified time.

    plan to play a sport in the future at an approximate time.

    haven't played a sport in a certain amount of time.

_____

_____

_____

_____

_____

_____

Preparation 熱身

Useful Vocabulary

打算	dǎsuàn	V	to plan
旅遊	lǚyóu	V	to travel (cf. 旅行)
加州	Jiāzhōu	N	California
打折	dǎzhé	V	to give a discount
而且	érqiě	Conj	furthermore, moreover

Can you figure out what U.S. cities these are? Try to guess by sound or meaning.

芝加哥 _____   丹佛 _____   波士頓 _____

西雅圖 _____   小石城 _____   邁阿密 _____

洛杉磯 _____   達拉斯 _____   華盛頓 _____

If you were recommending places that foreign students should visit while they are living in the States, which of these would you recommend and why?

Smithsonian Museum	斯密生博物館 (Sīmìshēng bówùguǎn)
Statue of Liberty	自由女神像 (Zìyóunǚ shén xiàng)
Disneyland	迪斯尼樂園 (Dísīní lèyuán)
Liberty Bell	自由鐘
Yellowstone National Park	黃石公園
Rocky Mountain Park	落磯山脈 (Luòjīshānmài)
Grand Canyon	大峽谷 (Dàxiágǔ)
The U.S. Capitol	美國國會大廈 (xià)

What other places might you suggest? Why?

_____

_____

Indicate which of the following terms you think refer to men and which refer to women. Then write the letter of the definition for these general family terms. (NOTE: Keep in mind that sometimes other factors such as regional differences and distinctions in age or marital status may affect the terms used for certain family members.) Several entries have already been done for you.

男	女	_c_ 舅舅 jiùjiu	a. 母親的姐妹
男	女	_a_ 阿姨 āyí	b. 舅舅的母親
男	女	___ 姑姑 gūgu	c. 母親的哥哥弟弟
男	女	_f_ 叔叔 shūshu	d. 父親的姐妹
男	女	___ 伯伯 bóbo	e. 舅舅的太太
男	女	___ 舅媽 jiùmā	f. 父親的弟弟
男	女	___ 外婆 wàipó	g. 父親的哥哥

▶ Listening for the Gist 泛聽

The main topic of this conversation is:

- ❑ Xiao Zhang's plans for a family vacation
- ❑ The cost of traveling in the United States
- ❑ Historical places in the U.S. Xiao Zhang and his family should visit before they return to China
- ❑ Whether Xiao Zhang and his family should drive or fly on their vacation
- ❑ Where Li Wenying has relatives living in the U.S.

What kinds of suggestions does Li Wenying make?

_____

_____

_____

▶ Listening for Details 靜聽

How much was Xiao Zhang planning to spend on airfare?

_____

How much are the tickets Xiao Li knows about?

_____

他們家爲什麼要去加州?
- ❑ 要看李文英的舅舅和舅媽。
- ❑ 要省錢。
- ❑ 小張的女兒沒去過迪斯尼樂園。
- ❑ 小張沒時間帶她女兒去玩。
- ❑ 小張覺得加州的天氣最好。

李文英爲什麼提到她的舅舅? (check all that apply)
- ❑ 他住在洛杉磯。
- ❑ 小張的女兒可以跟他們家的孩子玩。
- ❑ 他家離迪斯尼樂園非常近。
- ❑ 張林生可以住在他家。
- ❑ 小李要請小張把東西交給他。
- ❑ 他可以幫小張的忙。

Key Language Points 語言點

掉 diào

The basic meaning of 掉 is to fall or to drop down.

Examples:

我每次看那個電影都掉眼淚。 (yǎnlèi: tears)

到了冬天樹葉子都掉了。 (yèzi: leaves)

掉 + 在 means to fall or drop to a certain place.

Examples:

書掉在地下。

那個小孩的手套 (shǒutáo: gloves) 掉在路上。

掉 can also mean to omit or to lack.

Example:

這句話掉了一個字。

Verb + 掉 + 了 (resultative complement) indicates that the action of the verb has been accomplished.

In this conversation Zhang Linsheng said "我的汽車已經賣掉了." Complete these sentences using one of the verbs given below + 掉. Then translate each sentence into English.

忘   吃   壞   賣   跑   走

1. 小李本來要五點鐘給她舅舅打電話，可是她_____了。

_____

_____

2. 張林生的女兒跟她的小朋友把蛋糕都_____了。

_____

_____

3. 小張要買很便宜的飛機票，可是他聽說那種票早就_____了。

_____

_____

4. 李文英打算做麻婆豆腐，可是豆腐已經＿＿＿＿＿＿＿了。

_____

_____

5. 昨天小張找買他汽車的人，可是他＿＿＿＿＿＿＿了。

_____

_____

Interrogative words are sometimes used in an indefinite sense to mean "whichever one," "whatever," "wherever," etc. When Xiao Li asks Xiao Zhang: "有沒有決定坐哪家航空公司？" he responds by saying: "哪家航空公司便宜就坐哪家." How would you translate his response?

_____

_____

Answer these questions using interrogative words in each case. In some instances you are given hints in parentheses.

1. 他們打算買哪天的飛機票？

_____

2. 坐飛機的時候他們要坐哪兒？（位子，空）

_____

3. 他們要在迪斯尼樂園看什麼？（有意思）

_____

4. 他們在加州的時候要吃什麼樣的飯？（方便）

_____

Follow-up Activities 應用

大家來說 Role-Playing (Oral)

After talking it over with his family and getting the flight information from Xiao Li, Xiao Zhang decided to call a travel agent to help him book the best and cheapest flight. Enact this conversation with a partner.

大家來寫 Role-Playing (Written)

It's not surprising that Zhang Linsheng's daughter wants to go to Disneyland. Disney products and movies are well advertised and readily available in many parts of China and Taiwan. Recently Zhang Linsheng's friend sent him a photograph of a new shopping district in Suzhou (located near a famous temple). Imagine you are going to interview five of the people in the area about their attitudes toward having a Disney store right there and the impact this has on Chinese culture.

Write your questions in Chinese here:

1. _____

_____

2. _____

_____

3. _____

_____

4. _____

_____

5. _____

Preparation 熱身

Useful Vocabulary

Identify the following pictures using the appropriate Chinese characters:

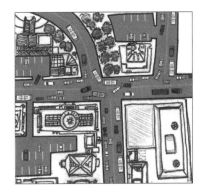

_____   _____   _____

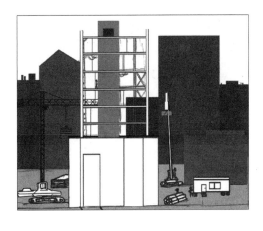

_____   _____

蓋房子　gài fángzi　　　拆房子　　chāi fángzi　　　到處都是人

高樓　　gāolóu　　　　交通很亂　luàn (塞車 sāichē)

Additional Useful Vocabulary

變化	biànhuà	N	change(s)
到處	dàochù	Adv	everywhere
想像	xiǎngxiàng	V/N	to imagine, imagination
乾淨	gānjìng	Adj	clean (opposite 髒 zāng, dirty)
氣候	qìhòu	N	weather, climate
愛	ài	V	to love, to be fond of (opposite 恨 hèn: to hate)
污染	wūrǎn	V/N	to pollute, pollution (空氣污染 kōngqìwūrǎn: air pollution)

▶ Listening for the Gist 泛聽

Who is originally from Beijing? (circle one)

李文英   張林生

Who just returned from Beijing? (circle one)

李文英   張林生

What are some of the changes in Beijing that are mentioned in this conversation? (check all that apply)

❑ More pollution   ❑ More high rise buildings

❑ Increase in traffic   ❑ Worse weather

❑ More new construction   ❑ Greater unemployment

❑ Higher standard of living   ❑ More restaurants

❑ More people have cars

▶ Listening for Details 靜聽

How long has it been since Zhang Linsheng was in Beijing?

_____

_____

What season does he remember as having the best weather?

□ 夏天　　　□ 冬天　　　□ 秋天　　　□ 春天

Write in pīnyīn and/or Chinese characters the two comments Xiao Li makes about the weather.

1. _____

_____

2. _____

_____

Key Language Points 語言點

When Li Wenying's parents asked her about her studies in the U.S., here's what she said: "Studying Chinese literature in America is really different from what I imagined." How would you translate her response into Chinese? (Remember Zhang Linsheng's comment about Beijing? He said "跟我想像的北京可不太一樣了.")

_____

_____

Using the phrase "到處都是…," describe the following places:

北京的火車站

_____

香港的購物中心

_____

迪斯尼樂園

_____

北京大學的圖書館

_____

上海的飯館

_____

臺北的動物園

_____

連連看 Draw lines connecting the antonyms:

原來	恨
蓋	冷
乾淨	平房
熱	拆
高樓	髒
愛	現在

Write complete sentences in the spaces provided on the next page using a subject + verb + resultative 得 from Column A and the result from Column B. Then translate each sentence into English. The first sentence has been done for you.

Column A	Column B
李文英熱得	不敢出門
交通亂得	非常厲害
高樓蓋得	誰都不高興
空氣污染厲害得	連公共汽車也不能走
天氣冷得	滿頭大汗
車子塞得	應該多穿一點衣服
小李熱得	越多越好

Example:

1. 李文英熱得不敢出門。

   Li Wenying was so hot she wouldn't dare go outside.

2. _____

   _____

3. _____

   _____

4. _____

   _____

5. _____

   _____

6. _____

   _____

7. _____

   _____

Follow-up Activities 應用

大家來說 Role-Playing (Oral)

That evening Xiao Zhang and his wife talked about the ways in which Beijing has changed. His wife Liu Zhen 劉珍 is from a small town in the countryside in Hunan. According to her, things haven't really changed there that much. Below are some pictures of the area around her hometown. Create a conversation based on these photos with a partner.

大家來寫 **Role-Playing (Written)**

What do you think are some reasons why China has changed so much in the past ten years? Write a short paragraph in which you discuss at least three of these factors.

_____

_____

_____

_____

_____

_____

_____

_____

_____

_____

_____

_____

_____

Preparation 熱身

Useful Vocabulary

Identify the following items using the appropriate Chinese characters:

電子郵件	傳眞機 chuánzhēnjī
文件	護照 hùzhào
機票	簽證 qiānzhèng

Additional Useful Vocabulary

道別	dàobié	VO	to say goodbye (formal; implies a long separation)
超重	chāozhòng	V	to exceed the weight limit
檢查	jiǎnchá	V	to examine
換錢	huànqián	V	to change money
保持	bǎochí	V	to maintain, to keep
聯繫	liánxì	V/N	to maintain contact; to connect (cf. 聯絡 liánluò: to contact); contact, connection

When is it appropriate to say: 祝你一路順風?

_____

_____

What arrangements do you need to make ahead of time if you are planning to fly to China or Taiwan?

_____

_____

What do you need to do when you get to the airport?

_____

_____

▶ Listening for the Gist 泛聽

Why does Zhang Linsheng call Li Wenying?
- ❏ To ask her to take him and his family to the airport
- ❏ To ask her advice about what time they should be at the airport
- ❏ To ask her how much baggage is allowed on international flights
- ❏ To say goodbye

What else do they talk about?

_____

_____

_____

_____

▶ Listening for Details 靜聽

Based on this conversation, complete this chart.

Day of departure	
Time plane departs	
Time they plan to arrive at the airport	
Time they will leave for the airport	

小李提醒小張到了中國以後

　□　給她打電話　　　　□　給她寫一封信

　□　給她寄電子郵件　　□　給她發傳真

Based on what Zhang Linsheng says, complete this sentence and translate it into English:

一般來說_____

_____

_____

Key Language Points 語言點

Check the best definition for 聯絡.

□ 有來往   □ 聊天   □ 旅遊   □ 慶祝

連連看 Draw lines connecting the antonyms.

接	回家
寄	見面
分開	忘記
道別	高興
記得	送
出門	受
難過	歡迎

* * *

一定不要(別) Strong Prohibitive: Definitely don't + verb

In this conversation Xiao Li reminded Xiao Zhang to make sure his family's luggage didn't exceed the weight allowed by the airlines.* When Xiao Zhang called his landlord to say goodbye, he was given a lot of travel advice by him too. Translate these concerns into Chinese:

Definitely do not …

… take too much luggage.

_____

… put a pocketknife (小刀) in your suitcase.

_____

… forget to bring some snacks to eat during the flight.

_____

… get to the airport too late.

_____

… forget to bring your passport and plane ticket.

_____

… take fruit into a foreign country.

_____

… forget to change money before you get on the plane.

_____

… smoke (抽煙 chōuyān) on the plane.

_____

*NOTE: Xiao Li said "一定不要把行李超重," but a more standard way of saying this is "一定不要讓行李超重."

Follow-up Activities 應用

大家來說 Role-Playing (Oral)

Before landing in Beijing, Xiao Zhang was given this customs form to fill out. Can you fill it out for him?

边防检查 **入境登记卡**

中国公民（含港澳台）填写
请使用中文填写，□ 内请划 ✓

姓　　名	男 □　女 □

官方使用

证件号码	出生日期　年　月　日
签注号码	国籍（地区）
签注签发地	中国 □（香港 □　澳门 □　台湾 □）
船名/车次/航班号	**入境事由**（只能填写一项）
来自何地	会议/商务 □　访问 □　现光/休闲 □ 探亲访友 □　就业 □　学习 □ 返回常住地 □　定居 □　其他 □
国内住址	

证件种类 □

以上申明真实完整。如有不实填报，愿承担由此引起的一切法律责任。

签名

入境日期　年　月　日

公安部出入境管理局监制
J(01.02)

A few days after Zhang Linsheng and his family arrived in Beijing he sent Li Wenying an email. In this message he talked about the flight, his impressions of Beijing, and what he has been doing since he returned to China. He also asked about what she's been doing. Imagine you are Zhang Linsheng and write this email message for him.

TO:　　　<u>Li Wenying</u>

FROM:　　Zhang Linsheng

RE:　　　wǒ dàole

Role-Playing (Telephone)

After Li Wenying received this email she called another classmate to talk about how Zhang Linsheng was doing. With a partner enact this conversation.

Preparation 熱身

Rewrite the Chinese characters from the next page under the appropriate pictures.

_____   _____   _____

_____   _____   _____

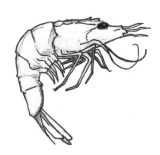

_____   _____   _____

海蝦	hǎixiā	牛肉	niúròu	魚	yú
啤酒	píjiǔ	生菜	shēngcài	雞腿	jītuǐ
菊花	júhuā	玫瑰花	méiguīhuā	西紅柿	xīhóngshì (PRC)
汽水	qìshuǐ	雞蛋	jīdàn		
牛奶	niúnǎi	番茄	fānqié (TW)		

Additional Useful Vocabulary

牌價	páijià	N	list price (PRC)
斤	jīn	N	unit of weight; ½ kilogram
束	shù	M	a bunch of
罐	guàn	N	a can (of soda, beer, etc.)
隻	zhī	M	for birds, some animals, one of a pair of things
枝	zhī	M	for long, thin objects (pens, cigarettes, etc.) and for flowers with stems intact
農民	nóngmín	N	farmer
稍微	shāowēi	Adv	slightly

You are planning to cook a meal tonight and so you need to go shopping. What kinds of food and drink would you expect to find at a public market? List five to eight items.

_____

_____

_____

_____

_____

_____

_____

▶ Listening for the Gist 泛聽

Who are the speakers in this conversation?
- ❑ Two customers
- ❑ A customer and a farmer
- ❑ Two farmers
- ❑ A reporter and a farmer

Which sections of this recording are repeated? (circle one)

One and two   Two and three   One and three

▶ Listening for Details 靜聽

Fill in the prices and the appropriate measure word for each item mentioned. Be careful —not all the items listed below are in the report.

海蝦	_____ 元 / _____	牛肉	_____ 元 / _____
草魚	_____ 元 / _____	啤酒	_____ 元 / _____
可樂	_____ 元 / _____	番茄	_____ 元 / _____
米	_____ 元 / _____	生菜	_____ 元 / _____
雞腿	_____ 元 / _____	白菜	_____ 元 / _____
玫瑰花	_____ 元 / _____	菊花	_____ 元 / _____
汽水	_____ 元 / _____	雞蛋	_____ 元 / _____
牛奶	_____ 元 / _____		

What is the man being interviewed selling today?

	✔		✔
牛肉		魚	
蝦		雞蛋	
番茄		生菜	
汽水		雞	
啤酒			

他賣的東西比以前...

	✔
稍微便宜了。	
便宜多了。	
稍微貴了。	
貴多了。	
一樣。	
他沒說。	

那是因為 ...

	✓
沒有人買他的東西。	
他沒有錢。	
幾個月以前下大雨了。	
幾個月都沒有下雨。	

Key Language Points 語言點

Some measure words function the same way in Chinese as in English. For example, in this recording you heard that in Chinese a can of soda is _____. Write the appropriate Chinese characters for the following. A list of possible measure words is given to get you started.

塊　本　枝　雙　碗　片　罐　條　瓶　束　張　杯　位　件

a cup of tea

_____

a slice of bread　（麵包 miànbāo）

_____

a pair of chopsticks　（筷子 kuàizi）

_____

a chunk of meat

_____

a bottle of wine

_____

a bowl of rice

_____

a bunch of flowers

_____

a can of beer

_____

Review some of the other measure words you have learned by writing the appropriate measure word for each of these nouns.

_____

_____

✳   ✳   ✳

At the end of the interview the reporter says to the farmer: 啊，是這樣嗎? How would you translate this question? Does it require an answer? Why or why not?

_____

_____

Think of two other situations when it might be appropriate to say this. On the next page, create two short dialogues in which this would be the final comment a person would say.

1. 甲: _____

_____

_____

乙: 啊，是這樣嗎？

2. 甲: _____

_____

_____

乙: 啊，是這樣嗎？

Follow-up Activities 應用

大家來說 Role-Playing (Oral)

Here are some photos taken that day at the public market. With a partner talk about each picture, making sure you describe what is being sold and how it is displayed.

大家來寫 **Role-Playing (Written)**

Now imagine that you overhear a conversation between one of the farmers and a customer. The customer has a number of items s/he wants to buy but first wants to know the price, wants to know if the food is fresh (xīnxiān 新鮮), and also needs some help knowing how much to buy. Of course it's always a good idea to bargain a little, too. Write down (in pīnyīn or characters) what this dialogue might be like.

_____

_____

_____

_____

_____

_____

_____

_____

_____

_____

_____

Preparation 熱身

Useful Vocabulary

燈籠	dēnglóng	N	lantern
掛	guà	V	to hang
小時	xiǎoshí	N	an hour (cf. 鐘頭)
不過	búguò	Conj	but, however (cf. 可是)
門口	ménkǒu	N	entrance

Do you like to plan activities with friends in advance or do you like to do things spontaneously? Think about the last time you initiated a plan to do something with someone and jot down whether you planned it for a long time, whether you ended up doing what you originally had in mind, and what you might want to do with that person the next time you get together. Do you think your attitude toward doing things with friends would be different if you were a student living in China? In what ways?

_____

_____

_____

_____

_____

_____

_____

▶ Listening for the Gist 泛聽

Who made the phone call? (Circle one.)

哈寧   英南

Who seems to be busier?

哈寧   英南

Haning and Yingnan planned to go…

❑ to the zoo   ❑ out to eat

❑ to the movies   ❑ to the museum

❑ rollerskating

▶ Listening for Details 靜聽

Check all the times that were mentioned.

	✓		✓
today		Saturday at noon	
this afternoon at 1:00		Saturday afternoon	
this evening		Sunday morning	
Saturday morning		Sunday at noon	
Sunday afternoon		Saturday 1:00 p.m	
Sunday 1:00 p.m.		tomorrow	

Yingnan was free to go on…

❑ Saturday morning   ❑ Sunday afternoon

❑ Saturday evening   ❑ Saturday at noon

Haning and Yingnan planned to meet…

❑ at the gate of the Beijing zoo   ❑ near Mao's mausoleum on Tian'anmen Square

❑ at the Dahua Theater   ❑ at the entrance to the New China Bookstore

Who says 不見不散?

Haning   Yingnan

What is the best translation for this comment?

	✓
If I don't see you I won't leave.	
Don't leave before you see me.	
I won't see you until I'm done.	

Key Language Points 語言點

What would be an appropriate response to the question 有沒有什麼事? (check all that apply)

	✓		✓
有一些事情。		有很多新衣服。	
沒什麼事。		很忙。	
找不到工作。		我都有空。	

* * *

Fill in the Chinese characters and pīnyīn for "Raise the Red Lantern."

漢字	pīnyīn
_____ _____燈籠_____高掛	dàhóng_____ _____gāo_____guà

Follow-up Activities 應用

大家來說 Role-Playing (Oral)

What do you like to do on the weekends? With a partner take turns inviting each other to join you in this activity (in Chinese). Be sure to find out if the person likes this activity, when you both are free, and where you will meet.

大家來寫 **Role-Playing (Written)**

Here is a weekly calendar. Make a note about the activity that Haning and Yingnan have planned in the "Things to do this week" section. Include all pertinent information in Chinese, i.e., date, time, meeting place, activity, etc. In addition, make appointments (in Chinese) with three different classmates and record them on the proper days at the proper time.

Planner	星期一		星期二	
	8:00		8:00	
	9:00		9:00	
	10:00		10:00	
	11:00		11:00	
	12:00		12:00	
	1:00		1:00	
	2:00		2:00	
	3:00		3:00	
	4:00		4:00	
	5:00		5:00	

Things to do this week	星期三		星期四	
	8:00		8:00	
	9:00		9:00	
	10:00		10:00	
	11:00		11:00	
	12:00		12:00	
	1:00		1:00	
	2:00		2:00	
	3:00		3:00	
	4:00		4:00	
	5:00		5:00	

Notes	星期五		星期六	
	8:00		8:00	
	9:00		9:00	
	10:00		10:00	
	11:00		11:00	
	12:00		12:00	
	1:00		1:00	
	2:00		2:00	
	3:00		3:00	
	4:00		4:00	
	5:00		5:00	

Preparation 熱身

Useful Vocabulary

沿	yán	V	to follow, to go along
側	cè	N	side
步行	bùxíng	V	to go on foot
動物園	dòngwùyuán	N	zoo
正	zhèng	Adv	precisely, exactly
對	duì	Adj	facing, opposite
米	mǐ	N	meter
標誌	biāozhì	N	sign, mark
石頭	shítou	N, Adj	stone
獅子	shīzi	N	lion (石獅子)
迷	mí	V	to lose one's bearings, to become confused (迷路)

When you ask someone for directions, do you visualize in your mind where you need to go? As an experiment, ask the person next to you for directions to the library. As they give you directions, sketch out a map in the space provided below. Switch roles when finished.

▶ Listening for the Gist 泛聽

The conversation is between…

	✓
two friends	
two strangers	
a passenger and a bus driver	
a mother and a daughter	

The woman is asking directions to…

	✓
the zoo	
a bus stop	
a bookstore	
a market	

Check all the places you heard mentioned in this conversation.

	✓
the market	
Beijing Xinhua Bookstore	
Nanhua Cafeteria	
#10 bus stop	
the zoo	
Beijing library	
Guangming Theater	

Check the different modes of transportation you heard mentioned.

	✓
bus	
car	
walking	
taxi	

▶ Listening for Details 靜聽

In order to arrive at her destination, Yingnan needs to follow the directions in the proper sequence. Number the instructions below in their proper order, according to the conversation.

	#
Get off the bus at the zoo	
Get on the #10 bus	
Walk straight ahead (left of the Beijing Library) for about five minutes	
Walk straight ahead (on the right side of the zoo) for 100 meters	
Look for the stone lions	

Key Language Points 語言點

The person giving directions uses the construction verb + 著 twice in her explanation. Here are the two passages in which these comments occur. Go back and listen to her directions and fill in the blanks accordingly. Some additional blank spaces have been left for you to fill in, too.

1. 你_____著這個北京圖書館，它的_____側，向前走，然後你就會看到一個_____站。

2. 下車以後你_____這個動物園大門口，它的_____側，再往前走一百米_____了。

Choose the letter of the word from Column B that is a synonym or definition for the word in Column A.

Column A	Column B
_____ 步行	a. 不遠
_____ 明白	b. 不多
_____ 向	c. 很
_____ 非常	d. 懂
_____ 很近	e. 往
	f. 走路

Follow-up Activities 應用

大家來說 Role-Playing (Oral)

On the map below, write in the Chinese characters for the street names. Then draw in the location of the bus station, the hotel, the hospital, and the market, using the symbols below the map. With a partner take turns asking where each place is located, starting at the arrow in the bottom right corner of the map.

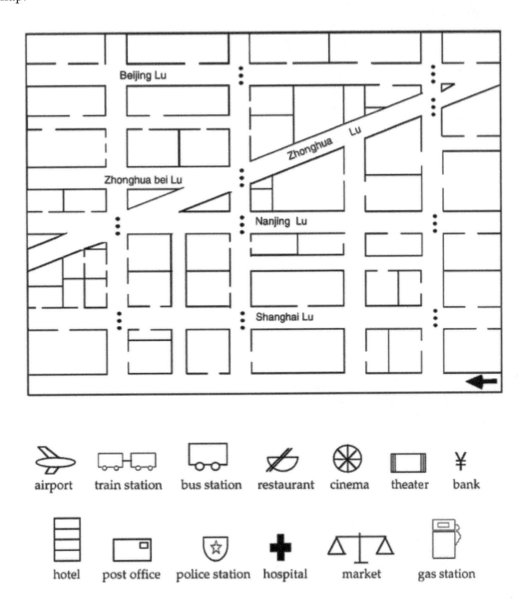

airport   train station   bus station   restaurant   cinema   theater   bank

hotel   post office   police station   hospital   market   gas station

大家來寫 Role-Playing (Written)

Below are two pictures of the West Entrance at Beijing University. In Chinese, list five interesting features you notice.

Preparation 熱身

Useful Vocabulary

搞	gǎo	V	(colloq.) to do, to work, to manage, etc.
反	fǎn	Adj	opposite
出發	chūfā	V	to set out
頭髮	tóufa, tóufǎ	N	hair
理髮店	lǐfādiàn, lǐfǎdiàn	N	hair salon (cf. 美容院 měiróngyuàn beauty parlor)
剪	jiǎn	V	to cut
排隊	páiduì	V	to stand in line
陪	péi	V	to accompany
回	huí	MW	for 事
		V	to return, go back

Draw a line connecting each Chinese expression to its English equivalent.

怎麼回事(兒)　　I'm sorry.

怎麼搞的　　Not bad!

對不起　　Is anything the matter?

沒關係　　Don't mention it; you're welcome.

真不錯　　What happened?

You made plans to meet a friend at a specific time, but you arrived late. What conversation might occur between you and your friend once you arrive? List five things that might be said.

_____

_____

_____

_____

_____

_____

_____

▶ Listening for the Gist 泛聽

Of the following topics, indicate which ones you heard mentioned in the dialogue:

	✓
Why Yingnan arrived later	
The time when Yingnan arrived	
Making an apology	
The location where they met	
The reason they got together	
The weather	
Wearing new clothes	
Getting a haircut	
Riding the bus	
Watching a movie	

▶ Listening for Details 靜聽

Please complete the following sentences according to what you heard in the dialogue. Put a check by the correct answer.

Yingnan was late because she…

	✓
lost track of time	
missed the bus	
took the wrong bus	
was getting a haircut	

Yingnan and Haning plan to…

	✓
go shopping	
have lunch together	
go see a movie	
get their hair cut	

They finally left together at…

	✓
12:00	
2:00	
2:35	
12:35	
5:35	

Who got a haircut?

Yingnan   Haning   Yingnan and Haning

Her/their haircut(s) cost…

	✓
$10.00	
$18.00	
$8.00	
$15.00	

Indicate who said the following lines by filling in the number under each name.

Yingnan said:	Haning said:

1. "我來晚了"。
2. "我那個車子坐錯了"。
3. "你今天的裙子很漂亮"。
4. "是新買的嗎"？
5. "你的頭髮很漂亮"。
6. "還其實不算太貴"。*
7. "人好多，都在排隊"。
8. "我陪你去"。
9. "那我們快點兒走吧"。
10. "來不及了吧"。

(*NOTE: Really she should have said "其實還不算太貴".)

* * *

英南上了幾路公共汽車？

☐ 四路車   ☐ 四十路車
☐ 十路車   ☐ 十四路車

Key Language Points 語言點

Provide subjects for these verb phrases based on what you heard in the dialogue. You can write in either pīnyīn or Chinese characters.

1. _____走錯了

2. ＿＿＿＿＿＿＿＿＿＿看完了

3. ＿＿＿＿＿＿＿＿＿＿反了

4. ＿＿＿＿＿＿＿＿＿＿走回來了

5. ＿＿＿＿＿＿＿＿＿＿新買的

6. ＿＿＿＿＿＿＿＿＿＿昨天剪的

7. ＿＿＿＿＿＿＿＿＿＿挺有名的

＊　＊　＊

Toward the beginning of this conversation Yingnan says "結果問了一個人." 結果 means "as a result, it ended up that." Complete the following sentences using 結果.

Example:

我本來要坐十九路車，結果

↳　我本來要坐十九路車，結果坐了十路車，坐錯了。

1. 哈寧昨天説她不要剪頭髮，結果⋯

＿＿＿＿＿＿＿＿＿＿＿＿＿＿＿＿＿＿＿＿＿＿＿＿＿＿＿＿＿＿＿＿＿＿

2. 英南告訴她男朋友她很喜歡這條裙子，結果⋯

＿＿＿＿＿＿＿＿＿＿＿＿＿＿＿＿＿＿＿＿＿＿＿＿＿＿＿＿＿＿＿＿＿＿

3. 哈寧跟英南12:50才到了電影院，結果⋯

＿＿＿＿＿＿＿＿＿＿＿＿＿＿＿＿＿＿＿＿＿＿＿＿＿＿＿＿＿＿＿＿＿＿

Follow-up Activities 應用

大家來說 Role-Playing (Oral)

Later that day Haning got her hair cut, did some shopping, and ran a few other errands. A friend of hers stopped by to visit in the evening. Enact their conversation as they talked about what they each had done recently. Be sure to use at least the following vocabulary items:

隨便　　　結果　其實　頭髮　排隊 time word 才 verb

怎麼搞　　的　　剪　　回來　來不及

大家來讀 Role-Playing (Reading)

While Haning was waiting to get her hair cut, she read about a new book club that is being organized in Hong Kong and decided to fill out an application form. How would you fill out this form? Below is the form and some hints to help you out.

書會入會申請表格
中文姓名＿＿＿＿＿＿＿＿＿＿＿＿性別＿＿＿＿
英文姓名＿＿＿＿＿＿＿＿＿＿＿＿＿＿＿＿＿
職業＿＿＿＿＿＿＿＿＿＿教育程度＿＿＿＿＿
年齡（請在口加✓）　　口 24歲以下　口25歲-30歲 口 31歲-40歲　　口 41歲-50歲　口50歲以上
地址＿＿＿＿＿＿＿＿＿＿＿＿＿＿＿＿＿＿＿
＿＿＿＿＿＿＿＿＿＿＿＿＿＿＿＿＿＿＿＿＿
電話＿＿＿＿＿＿＿＿＿圖文傳真＿＿＿＿＿＿
E-MAIL：＿＿＿＿＿＿＿＿＿＿＿＿＿＿＿＿＿

閱讀興趣		
（請在口加✓，最高限選 5 類，如全部均有興趣需填1類）		
01口全部	02口哲學	03口社會科學、政治
04口經濟	05軍事	06口法律
07口文學、教育	08藝術	09口語言、文字
1A口中國文學	1B外國文學	11口歷史、文化、考古
12口地理	13口自然科學	1C口中醫
1D口西醫	15口工程技術	16口農林、畜牧、魚
17口綜合參考(年鑒百科全書)		18口體育、健身、保健
19口生活、娛樂	20口旅遊	21口兒童讀物
22口連環圖	57口字典詞典	59口線裝書
60口書冊圖書	62口紅學研究	63口魯迅研究

申請入簽署
口本人願意加入好文書會、享用書會提供給會員的專有服務，並付上劃線支票/銀行本票港幣/美元/加元/英鎊/奧元＿＿＿＿＿＿元，付好文書會年費。
簽署：   X 　　　　　　　　　　日期：

Helpful Vocabulary

性別	xìngbié	N	sex, gender
職業	zhíyè	N	occupation
教育程度	jiàoyùchéngdù	N	level of education
以下/以上	yǐxià/yǐshàng	Suf	below; under/above; over
限	xiàn	V	to set a limit, to restrict
類	lèi	N	categories
服務	fúwù	N	service
支票	zhīpiào	N	check
填	tián	V	to fill out (填表 tiánbiǎo: to fill out a form)

Answer the following questions in English based on this form.

1. Where should you write your address and fax number?

_____

_____

2. In the second section, under what circumstances should you check the box marked "01"?

_____

_____

3. What is the greatest number of categories you are advised to check?

_____

_____

4. If you were interested in dictionaries, which box would you check? _____

    How about Chinese medicine? _____

    Economics? _____   Linguistics? _____

    Natural science? _____   Travel? _____

    Archaeology? _____

5. What different types of currency are mentioned in the third section of the form?

_____

_____

6. If you check the box in the third section, what do you need to circle and what do you need to fill in?

_____

_____

7. If you sign, date, and mail in this form, what have you agreed to?

_____

_____

Preparation 熱身

Useful Vocabulary

帶	dài	V	to have something attached, to take, to carry
盥洗室	guànxǐshì	N	washroom
浴缸	yùgāng	N	bath tub
商量	shāngliang	V	discuss, talk over
拜託	bàituō	V	trouble someone with, request someone do something

Idiomatic Phrases

那就算了　　"Then forget it."　　"Then it's okay."

這樣吧　　"How about this?"　　"Let's do it this way."

When apartment hunting, what factors do you take into consideration? What features do you look for? List five of your concerns below.

_____

_____

_____

_____

_____

▶ Listening for the Gist 泛聽

Which of the following topics did Yingnan and Haning mention in this conversation?

	✓
The favor Yingnan requests	
Where she wants to find an apartment	
Where she is currently living	
The amount she can afford to pay for rent	
Why she plans to move	
Whether she wants an apartment with a private kitchen	
Whether she wants an apartment with a private bathroom	
Whether she wants an apartment with a bathtub	
When she plans to move	
The number of bedrooms she wants	

Does Haning seem able to help Yingnan find an apartment? How can you tell?

_____

_____

▶ Listening for Details 靜聽

Circle whether the statement is true (是) or false (非):

Yingnan wants a two-bedroom apartment.   是　非

Yingnan thinks 250 RMB is too much to pay for rent.   是　非

Yingnan thinks it would be best to have an apartment with a kitchen.   是　非

Yingnan does not really need a bathtub in the apartment.   是　非

Haning thinks Yingnan could get a one-bedroom apartment for 250 RMB.   是　非

How does Haning offer to help Yingnan find an apartment?

	✓
Take her to see an apartment	
Introduce her to someone she knows who has a vacant apartment	
Introduce her to someone she knows whose job is apartment rentals	

When are they planning to leave?

	✓
Right now	
After lunch	
After they call Haning's friend	
After they call about the apartment	

Key Language Points 語言點

In this conversation Yingnan says: 我有一件事情要拜托你. How would you translate this sentence?

_____

In Chinese there are many polite ways to ask for someone's assistance or to get their attention. 請問 and 對不起 ("excuse me," "pardon me") are most common and least formal and are often followed by a question of substance (e.g., 請問, 現在幾點鐘?). 拜托 is more limited in usage; it is used when someone is asking someone to do a favor. 勞駕 láojià, an expression used by northern Chinese speakers, is similar to 拜托.

Sometimes 麻煩 is used as a polite way of asking someone to do something, i.e., "May I trouble you to …" But it has many other meanings.

麻煩 máfan   V   to trouble, to disturb (cf. 打擾 dǎrǎo: to disturb [more formal than 麻煩)
              Adj   troublesome, bothersome
              N   trouble, annoyance

Examples. See if you can translate these sentences into English.

1. 英南覺得找房子眞麻煩。

_____

2. 她不願意麻煩哈寧，可是她沒有別的辦法。

_____

3. 她說我以後不會給你很多麻煩。

_____

Now fill in the blanks using one of the following terms. In some cases there is more than one correct answer.

拜托　　　麻煩　　　請問　　　對不起

1. 我想_____你一件事。

2. 哈寧非常願意幫英南的忙，她覺得一點也不_____。

3. _____，你有時間陪我找房子嗎？

4. 如果不太_____，你可不可以送我回家？

5. 請你幫我一個忙。_____ _____。

6. _____，你可不可以帶我去看一個房子。

7. _____你把那張地圖給我。

8. 住在沒有廚房的公寓太_____。

9. _____，這個公寓的盥洗室帶不帶浴缸？

10. 哈寧的朋友今天有一點不舒服，你最好別_____她。

Cross out the one word in this group that is not a near synonym.

前後	qiánhòu
左右	zuǒyòu
早晚	zǎowǎn
差不多	chàbuduō
上下	shàngxià

Follow-up Activities 應用

The next day Yingnan went to look at two apartments. Fill in the information to complete these advertisements based on the floor plans described. Based on what Yingnan said in her conversation with Haning, which apartment would she probably choose?

A _____   B _____

雅公寓租

寧靜，出入便. ＿＿＿
間臥室，大＿＿＿，
＿＿＿. 設全(電話，
冰箱，洗衣機，傢俱).
三佰五十. 夜 7:30 後
電六九六三八七五.

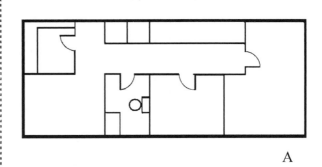

A

租. 女性單身. 近大學.
交便. 寧靜. 有＿＿間
臥室. 有＿＿＿，客廳.
設有電話，冰箱，＿＿＿.
二佰二十五. 電七七八
二二五六.

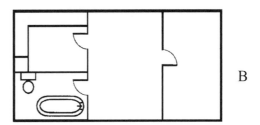

B

大家來說　Role-Playing (Oral)

Below is a photo of another apartment building that Yingnan looked at. With a partner, imagine that you and she were looking at an apartment in this building and that you also thought of a list of questions to ask the landlord and some of the other tenants who live there.

Preparation 熱身

Useful Vocabulary

普通	pǔtōng	Adj	common, ordinary
家常菜	jiāchángcài	N	family-style dish, home cooking
打散	dǎsàn	V	to break up, to beat
擱	gē	V	to place, to add (cf. 放)
創造	chuàngzào	V	to invent, to create
燉	dùn	V	to marinate
嚐(一嚐)	cháng(yìcháng)	V	to taste
首先	shǒuxiān	Adv	first (in a series of things)
		Conj	in the first place, first of all
新鮮	xīnxiān	Adj	fresh
菊花	júhuā	N	chrysanthemum
乾	gān	Adj	dry
泡(開)	pào(kāi)	V	to soak, to steep (e.g., 泡茶)

▶ Listening for the Gist 泛聽

How many dishes did the cook prepare?

_____

Check which ingredients were mentioned.

❑ eggs	❑ salt	❑ tomatoes
❑ onions	❑ garlic	❑ sugar
❑ ginger	❑ chicken	❑ shrimp
❑ beef	❑ fish	❑ MSG
❑ wine	❑ cola	❑ vinegar
❑ oil	❑ soy sauce	

▶ Listening for Details 靜聽

In Chinese, give the name of each dish and list at least three ingredients that are in it.

_____

_____

_____

Which dish is an authentic Cantonese recipe?

_____

Which dish was invented by the cook being interviewed?

_____

Which dish is a family-style dish?

_____

Give the proper order for the steps for steaming a fish, based on the explanation given by this cook.

	#
把魚洗一洗	
幾分鐘就可以，不要蒸得太老	
把魚放進鍋裡蒸	
擱點鹽，糖跟醬油	
放上一點菊花	

If you are unable to find fresh chrysanthemum flowers, what can be substituted and how should they be prepared?

Key Language Points 語言點

Write the letter from Column B of the definition or synonym of each word in Column A.

Column A	Column B
_____ 普通	a. 想出新方法
_____ 簡單	b. 吃一口
_____ 首先	c. 第一
_____ 擱	d. 調味兒
_____ 別	e. 可以
_____ 創造	f. 放
_____ 行	g. 平常的；一般的
_____ 嚐一嚐	h. 不要
	i. 容易

＊　＊　＊

千萬不要/千萬別 "By all means don't"

The chef uses the expression 千萬不要 twice in this interview. Write down what she says exactly in Chinese:

千萬不要

_____

千萬不要

_____

Complete the dialogues with a sentence using 千萬不要 (or 千萬別) that makes sense based on the information given in the first speaker's comment sentence.

Example:

　　甲：我已經覺得很累了。

　　乙：那你千萬不要再跑了。

1.　甲：我母親昨天給我的錢快用完了。

　　乙：_____

2.　甲：這個菜本來很鹹。 (xián: salty)

　　乙：_____

3.　甲：過年的時候，我父母要請幾位客人吃飯。

　　乙：_____

4. 甲：那條魚好像不太新鮮了。

   乙：_____

5. 甲：炒飯的做法很簡單，可是我做得沒有你做得好。

   乙：_____

Follow-up Activities 應用

大家來説 Role-Playing (Oral)

With a partner take turns acting out and explaining in Chinese how to make at least one of the dishes described in this interview. Be sure to mention what ingredients are needed (材料) and how the dish should be prepared (做法).

大家來寫 Role-Playing (Written)

Interview someone you know who cooks Chinese food. Find out what his or her favorite dish to prepare (拿手菜 náshǒucài) is and write down the recipe in Chinese.

Name of the dish: _____

Name of the chef: _____

材料：

_____

_____

_____

_____

做法：

_____

_____

_____

_____

_____

Preparation 熱身

Write the Chinese characters below under the appropriate pictures.

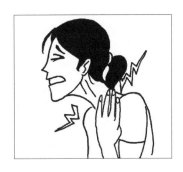

_____

_____

_____

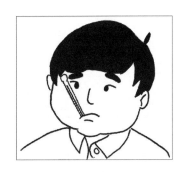

_____

_____

_____

_____

脈搏 màibó   舌頭 shétou   脖子 bózi   腦袋疼 nǎodài téng (頭疼)

疲勞 píláo   大夫 dàifu   體溫 tǐwēn

Useful Vocabulary

伸	shēn	V	to stretch out, to stick out (伸出來)
正常	zhèngcháng	Adj	normal
胃口	wèikǒu	N	appetite
趕	gǎn	V	to rush to finish, to rush to work on
論文	lùnwén	N	thesis, dissertation, research paper or article
睡眠	shuìmián	N	sleep
初期	chūqī	N	elementary, first stage
沖劑	chōngjì	N	medicine that needs to be mixed with water
袋	dài	N	packet
有效	yǒuxiào	V O	efficacious, effective, gets results (cf. 有用, 有效果 yǒu xiàoguǒ)

When you are ill, do you usually go to see a doctor? If so, what questions does the doctor ask you? If not, what kind of home remedies do you use? Do you make changes in your diet or other daily habits?

_____

_____

_____

_____

_____

_____

Write the letter from Column B of the definition or synonym of each word in Column A:

Column A	Column B
_____ 老（老是）	a. 一個星期
_____ 理解 lǐjiě	b. 非常累
_____ 腦袋	c. 氣力小
_____ 熬夜 āoyè	d. 醫生
_____ 弱 ruò	e. 經常
_____ 疲勞	f. 懂
_____ 一週	g. 深夜不睡覺
_____ 大夫	h. 頭

▶ Listening for the Gist 泛聽

Check all the topics mentioned in this conversation.

	✓
Where she doesn't feel well	
Whether she has a fever	
Whether she has been coughing	
Whether she is now taking any medicine	
What she normally eats	
What she normally drinks	
If she sleeps well	
If she gets regular exercise	
What her occupation is	

How would you describe this doctor's attitude toward his patient? Do you think the patient will follow his advice? Why or why not?

_____

_____

_____

▶ Listening for Details 靜聽

Check all that apply.

The patient was going to the doctor because she…

❑ had an accident   ❑ drinks too much coffee

❑ has a headache   ❑ has gastro-intestinal pains

❑ is tired

She was suffering from pain in…

❑ her shoulder

❑ her knee

❑ the left side of her head

❑ her eyes

She is experiencing the most discomfort…

❑ in the morning

❑ in the afternoon

❑ after meals

❑ in the evening

According to the doctor, she is ill because she…

❑ is not sleeping enough

❑ needs more fiber in her diet

❑ is drinking too much coffee

❑ has too much stress in her life

After identifying the patient's symptoms, the doctor diagnosed her as having…

❑ allergies   ❑ a cold

❑ a stomach ache   ❑ insomnia

The doctor advised her to…

❑ drink less coffee   ❑ sleep more

❑ rest more   ❑ take aspirin

❑ take digestive aids

The patient should take the medicine the doctor prescribed…

❑ once daily　　　❑ after meals

❑ twice daily　　　❑ three times daily

❑ as needed

How long should the patient wait to see if there is an improvement?

❑ A few days　　　❑ Ten days

❑ One week　　　❑ Two weeks

Key Language Points 語言點

多／少

In this conversation the doctor recommends that the patient do what more and what less? In both cases he uses the construction "subject 多／少 + verb."

_____

_____

Complete the following sentences using 多 or 少, depending on the context. Add whatever additional information is necessary to make the sentence complete.

Example:

　　　我今天非常餓，要_____一碗飯。

↳　　我今天非常餓，要多吃一碗飯。

1. 外邊很冷，你應該_____一點衣服。

2. 每天吃肉對身體不好。你應該_____一點。

3. 如果你體溫不正常的話，要_____。

4. 這本書只要八塊錢。你_____給了_____塊。

5. 趕論文的時候要_____喝_____。

多 and 少 are also used in other ways. See if you can translate these sentences into English and explain the function of each occurrence of 多 and 少.

1. 她以前病得很屬害，現在看起來好多了。

_____

_____

2. 本來有十六個學生要來吃飯，現在少了兩個。

_____

_____

3. 有的人説得多，做得少。

_____

_____

4. 今天飯做少了，恐怕不夠吃。

_____

_____

5. 我們是多年的老朋友了，我一定要請他吃飯。

_____

_____

6. 他們家什麼都有，什麼東西都不少。

_____

_____

7. 這個地方的天氣太糟糕，我不能在這兒長住。

_____

_____

8. 你少來這一套。 (yītào: phony promise, insincere gesture)

_____

_____

9. 你這個字多寫了一筆。

_____

_____

10. 請你多多指教。 (zhǐjiào: to instruct, polite expression for asking someone's criticisms)

_____

_____

＊　＊　＊

左右

When the doctor asks the patient about her temperature, what does she say (in Chinese)?

_____

How would you translate her statement?

_____

Here are some other ways of expressing approximation. In some cases these terms can be used synonymously.

1. 左右   zuǒyòu   around, more or less (used after numbers or after number + measure word)

2. 前後   qiánhòu   around, more or less; altogether

3. 上下　　　shàngxià　　　around, more or less

4. 差不多　　chàbuduō　　　almost, nearly

5. 幾乎　　　jīhū　　　　　almost

6. 差一點兒　chà(yi)diǎn(r)　almost

7. number + 來　　　　　　(used after 十, 百, 千, 萬) = approximately (cf. number+ 多)

8. 一般　　　yìbān　　　　most, in general

9. 大多數　　dàduōshù　　　the great majority

Fill in the blanks with the number(s) of the expression(s) from the list above that indicate(s) an approximation in each sentence. In some cases you will need to give more than one answer. Then translate the completed sentence.

1. 那個病人等了＿＿＿＿＿＿兩個小時。 (2 choices)

_____

2. 同時 (at the same time) 大概有十＿＿＿＿＿＿個人也在那兒等。

_____

3. 雖然這個醫院有＿＿＿＿＿＿三百個病房，可是＿＿＿＿＿＿的病人不住院。 (1 choice; 2 choices)

_____

4. ＿＿＿＿＿＿人都等到非常不舒服的時候，才找醫生看病。 (2 choices)

_____

5. 王大夫星期五非常忙，她＿＿＿＿＿＿忘了吃飯。 (2 choices)

_____

6. 那種藥相當貴，二十片要十八塊錢_____。

Follow-up Activities 應用

大家來寫 **Role-Playing (Written)**

Imagine that you are the doctor in this case. Take notes about this patient's condition in your medical journal. Make sure to include her symptoms, your diagnosis, what medication you prescribed, what advice you gave her, etc. Write in Chinese.

_____

_____

_____

_____

_____

大家來說 **Role-Playing (Oral)**

A few weeks later this patient was still not feeling well, so she went to see the doctor again. With a partner, act out this conversation. Make sure you at least use the following vocabulary items: 有效, 左右, 疲勞, 正常, subject 多／少+verb, 疼得… (or 痛得…), 熬夜, 睡眠, 弱, 休息.

Preparation 熱身

Useful Vocabulary

司機	sījī	N	driver
慌	huāng	Adj	to be anxious, upset, scared
衝	chōng	V	to collide, to crash
閃(開)	shǎn(kāi)	V	to avoid, to get out of the way
撞	zhuàng	V	to run into, to strike
受傷	shòushāng	V O	to receive an injury, to be injured
玻璃	bōlí	N	glass
失去知覺	shīqùzhījué	V O	to lose consciousness
流血	liúxuè, liúxuě	V O	to bleed (also pronounced xiě)
繫	jì	V	to fasten, to tie
安全帶	ānquándài	N	seat belt
幸虧	xìngkuī	Adv	fortunately
保險	bǎoxiǎn	N	insurance
		V	to insure
凹(進去)	wā, āo	Adj	sunken, dented, concave (cf. 凸 tū: protruding)
陷(進去)	xiàn	Adj	caved in, sunken
碎	suì	V	to be smashed
突然	tūrán	Adv	suddenly
拖	tuō	V	to haul away
幺	yāo	Nu	一, used orally for the numeral one

Have you ever been in a car accident? Were the police involved? If so, how did they handle the situation? If you were a police officer in charge of investigating a traffic accident, what would you do when you first arrived on the scene?

_____

_____

_____

_____

_____

_____

_____

Circle the number of cars that were involved in the accident.

一   二   三

What kinds of questions did the policemen ask?

	✓
If her seatbelt was fastened	
If she used her blinker	
If she lost consciousness	
What happened	
If she was hurt	
If she had the license plate number of the other car	
If anyone else was hurt	
If she had been drinking	
If she is the owner of the car	
Personal information (name, where she lives, works, etc.)	
If she needs to go to the hospital	

Toward the end of the conversation, what information did the woman offer? (check all that apply)

	✓
Her telephone number	
The number on her driver's license	
The number of her license plate	
The license plate number of the other car	
The name of her insurance company	

▶ Listening for Details 靜聽

Check the appropriate box based on the information in this conversation.

	Wang Hong's car	The red car
On Beijing Rd		
On Zhongshan Rd		
Stopped at the red light		
Ran through the red light		
Restarted when the light turned green		
Turned right on Beijing Rd		
Turned left on Zhongshan Rd		
Was hit from the left		
Was hit from the right		

Indicate the location of vehicle(s) when the accident occurred and the direction of travel:

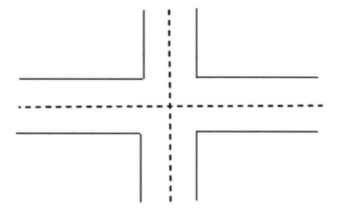

Horizontal: _____ Road   Vertical: _____ Road

Number of damaged area(s) of the vehicle: _____

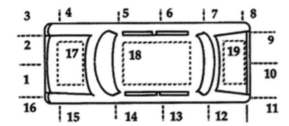

Based on the information given in the conversation, complete the investigator's traffic accident report.

INVESTIGATOR'S TRAFFIC ACCIDENT REPORT

Date of Accident: _____   Time: _____

City: _____   Investigator's Name: _____

Investigated at Scene: Y   N

Number Killed: _____   Number Injured: _____

Location: _____ Road(s)

Total Vehicle(s) Involved: _____

Driver's Name: _____   Sex: M   F

Office (dānwèi): _____   Phone: _____

Driver's Lic. No.: _____   Date of Birth: _____

Violation(s):   Y   N   (if yes) _____

Lic. Plate No.: _____   Body Type: _____

Insurance Policy #: _____

Vehicle Towed: Y   N

Wang Hong had to fill out an insurance form giving the details of the accident. As you can imagine, she was still somewhat shaken up by the experience and so she left out quite a few words. Can you help her complete the report? Use Chinese characters.

我把車_____在_____路的_____燈前。大概過了_____分鐘，換成了_____燈，我就_____拐，拐進_____路。突然，一輛_____色的車從我的_____邊直衝過來。我來_____及閃開，就被它撞了。

Key Language Points 語言點

Here are some excerpts from this conversation. First indicate who the speaker of each line is (male or female) and then indicate what the conversational function of the line is (choose the number of the functions listed below). For example, is the speaker trying to get information, offer advice, ask for clarification, etc.?

Conversational Functions

1. advising/suggesting

2. asking for information

3. assuming

4. giving an order

5. reaching a conclusion

6. denying

7. complying with a request

8. answering a question/giving information

9. repeating

10. requesting clarification

11. asking for advice

男　女　走開!走開!車禍有什麼好看呢? 都走開!　＿＿＿＿＿＿＿＿

男　女　你是這輛車的司機嗎?　＿＿＿＿＿＿＿＿

男　女　對，我就開這輛車。　＿＿＿＿＿＿＿＿

男　女　你的姓名?　＿＿＿＿＿＿＿＿

男　女　我叫王紅。　　　　　　　　　　　　_____

男　女　請你講一下車禍發生的經過。　　　_____

男　女　當時應該是他們那邊的紅燈。　　　_____

男　女　但是他沒有停…　　　　　　　　　_____

男　女　啊，他沒有停。　　　　　　　　　_____

男　女　當時他的速度很快？　　　　　　　_____

男　女　對。　　　　　　　　　　　　　　_____

男　女　有沒有失去知覺？　　　　　　　　_____

男　女　這倒沒有。　　　　　　　　　　　_____

男　女　還是去醫院檢查一下吧。　　　　　_____

男　女　那我現在怎麼辦？　　　　　　　　_____

男　女　你有沒有買保險呢？　　　　　　　_____

男　女　買了。　　　　　　　　　　　　　_____

男　女　請你把你保險卡拿出來讓我看一看。_____

男　女　喏，這是我（的）保險卡。　　　　_____

男　女　我們會儘快跟你聯繫的。　　　　　_____

Now write six sentences (three that might be spoken by the male speaker and three by the female speaker) that each show a different one of these conversational functions. Using the numbers above, indicate which function it is. Try to use as much of the following vocabulary as you can: 單位, 幸虧, 受傷, 衝, 慌, 安全帶, 突然, 撞.

Example:

男: 這輛車是你自己的嗎？ 2 (asking for information)

1. _____

2. _____

3. _____

4. _____

5. _____

6. _____

Follow-up Activities 應用

大家來說 Role-Playing (Oral)

When Wang Hong got home that night she called her parents and told them what had happened. Enact this conversation with a partner. Be sure to use the following vocabulary items: 幸虧, 受傷, 失去知覺, 速度, 衝過來, 慌得很, 撞, 玻璃, 閃開, 繫, 流血, 開不了, 保險公司.

大家來寫 Role-Playing (Written)

Imagine that you were a pedestrian who witnessed Wang Hong's accident. Using Chinese, write a paragraph describing in as much detail as possible exactly what you saw happen. Remember that this will become part of the accident file, so try to be precise.

_____

_____

_____

_____

_____

_____

_____

_____

_____

Preparation 熱身

Useful Vocabulary

旅行團	lǚxíngtuán	N	travel agency
游覽	yóulǎn	V	to go sight-seeing, to tour
安排	ānpái	V	to arrange
集合	jíhé	V	to gather, to meet up, to assemble
紀念品	jìniànpǐn	N	souvenir
突然	tūrán	Adv	suddenly
盒飯	héfàn	N	box lunch (cf. 飯盒, 便當)
地道	dìdào	Adj	genuine, authentic
行動	xíngdòng	N	movements, actions
老人家	lǎorénjiā	N	elderly people
設施	shèshī	N	facilities
自動	zìdòng	Adj	automatic
電梯	diàntī	N	elevator
嬰兒	yīng'er	N	baby, infant
寄存處	jìcúnchù	N	place to check things in

Imagine you are going to spend your holiday at a theme park (主題樂園). Below is a map of its concourse. List five activities you would like to do when you are there.

_____

_____

_____

_____

_____

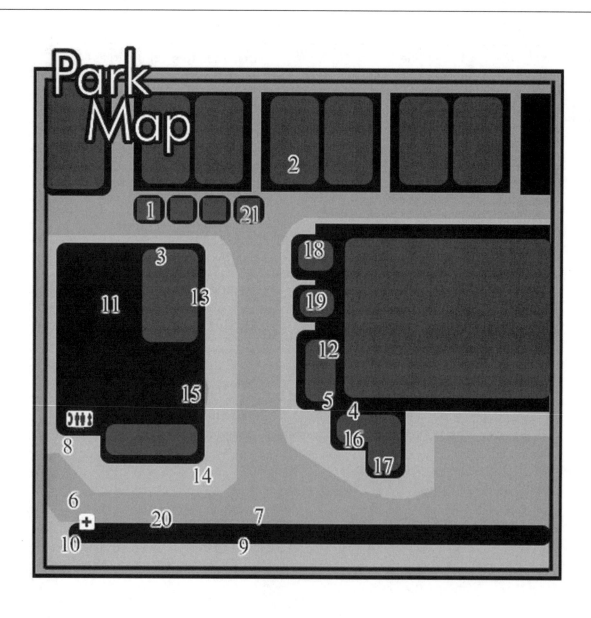

1。看看導演如何拍攝這部賣座電影然後感覺現場溫度達一萬度的大火爆發場面

2。看看我們的回到未來節目背後的電子特殊效果是如何製造出來的。也看看緊張大師的驚險刺激是怎麼來的

3。進去參觀電視劇第一皇后的事業歷程

4。快！挑上可以飛上星際的摩托車！然後一起和大頭哥哥飛到他的家。開始出乎想象的歷險幫助他的朋友和家人拯救他們的星球

5。一窺明目世界登峰造極的錄影區，觀眾可以參與其中

6。片廠有軌遊覽車入口處
7。電梯
8。往娛樂中心交通工
9。寄存嬰兒推車
10。警衛處

DINING
11。Park Commissary
12。Soft Serve Ice Cream
13。Bar
14。點心停

SHOPPING
15。Park Store
16。Toy Store
17。Alien Photo Spot
18。Amazing Pictures
19。Boutique
20。電影
21。Souvenir Shop

▶ **Listening for the Gist** 泛聽

The people who talked on the phone were…

	✓
a tourist and a bus driver.	
a tour guide and a tourist.	
the concierge at a hotel and a hotel guest.	
a travel agent and a tour guide.	

Did Mr. Wang already have some information about this tour? How do you know?

_____

_____

Who does Mr. Wang say he will go to the park with?

	✓
His wife	
His son or daughter	
His students	
Some friends	
His parents	
A group of tourists from China	

▶ Listening for Details 靜聽

Help Mr. Wang complete the following table based on what you heard in the recording:

Time	Place (no. on the map)	Activity
10:30 a.m.	#	
10:45 a.m.	#	
	#	
11:45 a.m.	#	
12:15 a.m.	#	

In English, list three things Mr. Wang is concerned about regarding this tour:

1. _____

2. _____

3. _____

陳小姐提到了哪些設施?

設施	提到了	沒提到
飯館		
電話亭		

設施	提到了	沒提到
電梯		
游覽車		
嬰兒車寄存處		
警衛處		

How did Ms. Chen translate the title of the movie *ET*? _____

What special attractions did she mention that pertain to the main character in this film?

_____

_____

旅行團為參加的人準備了什麼？ _____

要多少錢？ _____

Key Language Points 語言點

Fill in the blanks with one of the following phrases:

一下　　一類　　一些　　一起　　一個　　一張

1. _____ 地圖　　　　5. _____ 小吃店

2. _____ 問題　　　　6. 跟我們 _____ 去

3. _____ 影視效果　　7. 自動電梯 _____ 的東西

4. 問 _____

＊　　＊　　＊

Supply an object (in Chinese) for the following verbs based on what was said in this conversation. In some cases there may be more than one correct answer.

1. 問＿＿＿＿＿＿＿＿

2. 看＿＿＿＿＿＿＿＿

3. 買＿＿＿＿＿＿＿＿

4. 坐＿＿＿＿＿＿＿＿

5. 安排＿＿＿＿＿＿＿＿

6. 參加＿＿＿＿＿＿＿＿

7. 存＿＿＿＿＿＿＿＿

8. 準備＿＿＿＿＿＿＿＿

9. 幫助＿＿＿＿＿＿＿＿

10. 抱＿＿＿＿＿＿＿＿

Follow-up Activities 應用

大家來説 Role-Playing (Oral)

Mr. Wang's mother got separated from the rest of her family in the crowded toy store. Could you tell her how to rejoin them? (Sorry, she does not speak English.)

大家來寫 Role-Playing (Written)

Pretend you are writing a guide to the theme park for a group of students from China. Write an itinerary according to the park map. (Length: 50-100 Chinese characters.)

＿＿

＿＿

＿＿

＿＿

Preparation 熱身

Useful Vocabulary

羽毛球	yǔmáoqiú	N	badminton
訓練	xùnliàn	V, N	to train, training
比賽	bǐsài	V, N	to compete, competition
搭檔	dādàng	V, N	to be partners, partner
專業	zhuānyè	Adj, N	professional, specialty; major
謙虛	qiānxū	Adj	to be modest
規則	guīzé	N	rules, regulations (cf. 規矩, 規定)
差	chà	Adj	inferior, poor, weak
		V	to differ, to lack
差	chā	N	difference, discrepancy
愛好者	àihàozhě	N	fan (of sports, movie stars, etc.)
清惺	qīngxǐng	Adj	alert, wakeful
精力充分	jīnglì chōngfèn	Ph	full of energy
效率	xiàolǜ	N	efficiency, productiveness
徹底	chèdǐ	Adj	thorough
放鬆	fàngsōng	V	to relax, to be relaxed
按照	ànzhào	Prep	according to, on the basis of

▶ Listening for the Gist 泛聽

Check all the activities that Fang Ping and Wang Tao mention.

	✓		✓
swimming		bicycling	
badminton		pingpong	
basketball		tennis	
soccer		skiing	
jogging		ice skating	

What is each speaker's favorite sport to play?

Fang Ping	
Wang Tao	

What other topics are mentioned in this conversation?

	✓
Their personal experiences with professional athletic training	
The importance of diet and nutrition for athletes	
Their personal experiences with athletic competitions	
Their interest in watching competitive sports	
The benefits of exercise	
How hard it is to find time to exercise regularly	

▶ Listening for Details 靜聽

Based on the information in this conversation, complete these charts about Wang Tao and Fang Ping:

Wang Tao	
How often he practices	
Name of his partner	
Sport he learned as a child	

Wang Tao	
Age he learned this sport	
Who taught him?	
Types of training he received in China	
Did he compete in China?	
If so, at what level?	
Who will organize the upcoming competition?	
Will he participate?	
Other sports he regularly does	

Fang Ping	
How often she does this sport	
Age she learned this sport	
Who taught her?	
Types of training she received in China	
Did she compete in China?	
If so, at what level?	
Does she compete now?	
If so, at what level?	
Other sports she regularly does	

What is Fang Ping's attitude toward soccer? Why?

_____

_____

What is Wang Tao's attitude toward the Chinese soccer team? Why?

_____

_____

Number these phrases or sentences in the order they are spoken in the conversation and circle who the speaker is.

_____我才會覺得徹底放鬆。 王濤 方萍

_____我做運動也是這個目的。 王濤 方萍

_____運動完以後會覺得精力更加充分。 王濤 方萍

_____學習起來更有效率。 王濤 方萍

_____我們現在學習這麼緊張。 王濤 方萍

_____讓我的頭腦更清惺一點。 王濤 方萍

Key Language Points 語言點

Why does Fang Ping say "別謙虛"?

_____

_____

Think of a situation in which you might use this expression with one of your friends. Write this as a dialogue in Chinese below.

你的朋友： _____

你： 別謙虛！

* * *

愛好者　　fan: literally "one who is very fond of (sports/arts/movie stars, etc.)"
者　　　　a particle used in Classical Chinese that nominalizes what precedes it

Consider these compounds. Can you match the Chinese with the English equivalents?

記者   scholar

學者   reader

作者   writer

讀者   reporter

Do you remember the context in which Fang Ping uses the expression 學習緊張 xuéxíjǐnzhāng? Write a sentence with this phrase that relates to your own personal experience.

_____

✳ ✳ ✳

性   xìng   is added as a suffix to indicate -ty, -ness, -ility

In this conversation Fang Ping and Wang Tao spoke of sports competitions that were 全國性的. How would you translate this?

_____

Translate the following terms that have the suffix 性 added:

可能性 _____   實用性 _____

科學性 _____   可靠性 _____

創造性 _____   社會性 _____

時間性 _____

Follow-up Activities 應用

大家來說 Role-Playing (Oral)

That night Fang Ping's best friend from high school called from China. They had been on the swim team together for many years, and Zheng still swims competitively. Zheng was very curious about what kinds of sports Fang Ping is active in now, and Fang Ping is interested to hear about Zheng's experiences as a female athlete in China. With a partner, enact this conversation. Be sure to use at least the following vocabulary items:

訓練，徹底，規矩，比賽，謙虛，專業，緊張，複雜，全國性的

大家來寫 Role-Playing (Written)

Here's a picture of Wang Tao and his teammates practicing badminton at the student recreation center. You are a reporter for the school newspaper and you have just been given the assignment of interviewing this team and discussing their upcoming competition. Write down eight to ten questions that you plan to ask them at this interview.

_____

_____

_____

_____

_____

_____

_____

Preparation 熱身

Useful Vocabulary

區	qū	N	district
課程	kèchéng	N	curriculum
博士(學位)	bóshì (xuéwèi)	N	Ph.D.
棒	bàng	Adj (Coll)	非常好，了不起 (liǎobùqǐ)

Examples:

你研究中國的古典文學。你真棒。

這個電影很棒。我真想再看一次。

碩士(學位)	shuòshì (xuéwèi)	N	Master's Degree
學位	xuéwèi	N	degree
如此	rúcǐ	Adj/Adv	like this, as such, in this way
巧	qiǎo	Adj	coincidental
結實	jiēshí	Adj	strong
印象	yìnxiàng	N	impression

Examples:

我對他印象很好。

I have a good impression of him.

這個電影給我留下了深刻的印象。

That movie left a deep impression on me.

Go to a Chinese map website (e.g. Baidu) and find the section of the Beijing map that includes the following places. Print out this section of the map, find the locations and circle them.

Beijing Train Station 北京站

Palace Museum 故宫博物館

The Great Wall Restaurant 長城飯店

Tian'anmen Square 天安門

Chaoyang Rd. 朝陽路

Chaoyang District 朝陽區

Chairman Mao Memorial Hall 毛主席紀念堂

Tiantan (Temple of Heaven) Park 天壇公園

Eastern City District 東城區

Tiantan Hospital 天壇醫院

In meeting someone for the first time, what information would you expect to hear by way of introduction? How about if the person is from a foreign country? Jot down at least five things you might expect someone you are meeting for the first time to say or ask.

_____

_____

_____

_____

_____

▶ Listening for the Gist 泛聽

Which topics were mentioned by the woman in this conversation?

	✓		✓
Her name		Location of her home in the U.S.	
Her occupation in China		Reference to any family members in China	
Why she came to the U.S.		Whether she has children	
Her educational background		Her career plans	
Location of her home in China		Her plans for further education	

Toward the end of the conversation, the two speakers… (check all that apply)

	✓
exchanged phone numbers	
exchanged email addresses	
exchanged name cards	
None of the above	

▶ Listening for Details 靜聽

Based on the information given in this conversation, complete the chart.

Where Gao Lingyu 高玲玉 is from	
Her occupation in China	
Her current occupation	
How long she has lived in the U.S	
Where she grew up (name of neighborhood)	
Relatives mentioned	
Where Zhang Linsheng 張林生 is from	
Where he grew up (name of neighborhood)	
His current occupation	

What college did Zhang Linsheng attend?

	✓
Beijing University 北京大學 (北大)	
Beijing Normal University 北京師範大學 (北師大)	
Qinghua University 清華大學	
Beijing Industrial University 北京工業大學 (北工大)	

What college did Gao Lingyu attend?

	✓
北大	
北師大	
清華大學	
北工大	

Who is older? How do you know?

_____

_____

Why does he say that the two of them are 校友? What do you think this means?

_____

_____

What is the best translation for 我希望如此?

	✓
I hope so.	
I hope to do this.	
I hope you can do this.	
I hope I can be like you.	

Why does Gao Lingyu make this statement?

_____

_____

高玲玉説她將來要做什麼？

	✓
找比較好的工作	
回中國教書	
在美國念碩士學位	
在美國念博士學位	

高玲玉為什麼説她不太結實。這跟念書有什麼關係？

_____

Check the expression Gao Lingyu says at the end of the conversation. Now circle the other expression(s) that is/are synonymous with her comment.

保持聯絡   保持健康

保持聯繫   保重身體

Key Language Points 語言點

通 tōng is an extremely versatile verb that is used often in a range of contexts. The basic meaning is "to connect, to pass through." When 通 is duplicated it means "completely, thoroughly" (e.g., 北京的小地方他們通通知道). In this conversation Ms. Gao says, "我希望能夠通過碩士學位." What she means is that she hopes she can pass the exams (i.e., 碩士學位的考試) that will allow her to earn a Master's Degree. Can you figure out how 通 is used in these sentences? Translate each sentence into English.

1. 要是一個人説漢語，一個人説法文，他們的語言説不通。

_____

2. 那個小孩子一回家就跟父母通電話。

---

3. 這條小路通嗎?

---

4. 高老師跟她的朋友每個星期通一次信。

---

5. 新來的學生要通過語言考試才可以開始上課。

---

6. 這個字不通用了。

---

7. 那個小小的地方不通火車。

---

8. 他學中文好幾年了,一定是中國通。

---

9. 你為什麼不願意去中國留學? 我就想不通。

---

10. 一個字怎麼會有這麼多用法,我通通不懂。

Follow-up Activities 應用

大家來說 Role-Playing (Oral)

With a partner, imagine a situation in which you start talking to someone and then discover that you actually knew this person several years ago in a different place. Be sure to use at least the following vocabulary items:

真巧，世界真小，想不到，通，印象，好像，哪一天，聊一聊，保持聯繫。

大家來寫 Role-Playing (Written)

That night Zhang Linsheng wrote an email message in Chinese to his classmate Li Wenying and told her about the way he ran into Gao Lingyu. What do you think he said in this message?

From: Zhangls@abcmail.com
To: Liwenying@xyzmail.com
Subject: zhēnqiǎo

_____

_____

_____

_____

_____

_____

_____

Preparation 熱身

Useful Vocabulary

恰恰	qiàqià	Adv	exactly
相反	xiāngfǎn	Adj	opposite
嚴謹	yánjǐn	Adj	strict, rigorous
試驗	shìyàn	N	experiment
步驟	bùzhòu (bu zòu)	N	step, move
類似	lèisì	V	to be similar to
		Adj	similar, analogous
感受	gǎnshòu	V	to be affected by
		N	experience, feeling
創造力	chuàngzào lì	N	creativity
思維	sīwéi	N	thought, thinking
活躍	huóyuè	Adj	lively, animated (cf. huópo 活潑)
樂於	lèyú	V	to delight in, to take pleasure in
知音	zhīyīn	N	understanding friend, soul mate
典型	diǎnxíng	N	typical case, model
		Adj	typical, representative
無法	wúfǎ	VO	unable to, not to have the means to
驚喜	jīngxǐ	N	pleasant surprise
		V	to be pleasantly surprised

How would you describe the typical American student? Do you think you fall into this category? Why or why not?

_____

_____

_____

_____

_____

▶ Listening for the Gist 泛聽

Who has been in the U.S. longer?

Wang Tao   Sun Xiaohua

Which of the following characteristics of American students were mentioned in this conversation?

	✓		✓
They are polite.		They are creative.	
They study hard.		They are enthusiastic.	
They like to party.		They are aggressive.	
They are very thorough.		They are independent.	
They like to exercise.		They are lively.	
They are friendly.			

▶ Listening for Details 靜聽

Complete the chart based on the information given in this conversation.

Wang Tao		Sun Xiaohua	
How long has he been in the U.S.?		How long has she been in the U.S.?	
What is his major?		What is her major?	

Before coming to the U.S., what did Wang Tao think American students were like?

_____

_____

After coming to the U.S., how did his impressions change?

_____

_____

What does Sun Xiaohua find most remarkable about the students in her Chinese class?

_____

_____

When trying to figure out what a typical American is like, who did Sun Xiaohua ask?
- ❑ A Chinese friend
- ❑ One of the American students in her Chinese class
- ❑ An American friend
- ❑ One of the American teachers in the Chinese department
- ❑ One of the Chinese teachers in the Chinese department

Which of the following sentence(s) gives the same meaning as the comments made by the person who talked to Sun Xiaohua? (check all that apply)
- ❑ 我真的不能給你一個很正確的答案。
- ❑ 這個問題很難，我沒辦法回答。
- ❑ 我實在無法給你一個很準確的答案。
- ❑ 美國人的創造力非常強。
- ❑ 美國人要做什麼就做什麼。
- ❑ 美國人可以做他們心裡想做的事。
- ❑ 每個美國人都不一樣。

Did this person's explanation about "the typical American" make sense to Wang Tao? How do you know?

_____

_____

Key Language Points 語言點

Why does Sun Xiaohua say "你找到知音了"?

_____

What is another situation in which the term 知音 can be used? Write a brief dialogue in Chinese that you and one of your classmates might have in which you use this expression.

_____

_____

_____

＊　＊　＊

力 can be used as a suffix to indicate strength, power, movement, or force. In this conversation Sun Xiaohua spoke of her student's 創造力. Do you remember what she said?

_____

_____

Consider these examples of 力 functioning in this way:

記憶力　jìyìlì　　　　　memory

權力　　quánlì　　　　power, authority

功力　　gōnglì　　　　efficacy

重力	zhònglì	gravity
協力	xiélì	cooperation
説服力	shuōfúlì (PRC)	power of persuasion, persuasiveness
	shuìfúlì (TW)	

Now see if you can figure out what the following terms mean (try not to use a dictionary!):

馬力＿＿＿＿＿＿　　　能力＿＿＿＿＿＿　　　理解力＿＿＿＿＿＿

酒力＿＿＿＿＿＿　　　筆力＿＿＿＿＿＿　　　藥力＿＿＿＿＿＿

Follow-up Activities 應用

大家來説 Role-Playing (Oral)

With a partner discuss the ideas that Wang Tao and Sun Xiaohua mentioned about what a typical American student is. Do you agree with them? How would you describe the typical Chinese student? Do you think there are differences between students from the PRC and from Taiwan? Give examples to back up your opinions.

大家來寫 Role-Playing (Written)

After thinking further about this conversation, Wang Tao wrote a letter to a good friend in China who is planning to come study in the U.S. next year. He mentioned both what he himself had discovered about his American classmates as well as what he had learned from Sun Xiaohua and other friends. Help him write this letter. Be sure to use some of the new vocabulary from this lesson, such as 典型, 感受, 深刻, 創造, 類似, 樂於, 知音, 恰恰.

Preparation 熱身

Useful Vocabulary

熱鬧	rènào	Adj	lively, buzzing with excitement
小吃	xiǎochī	N	snacks
各地	gèdì	N	(各個地方)
建議	jiànyì	V	to advise, to recommend
冰	bīng	N	ice
燈	dēng	N	lantern, lamp
雕	diāo	V	to carve
根本	gēnběn	Adv	basically, fundamentally

Have you traveled to China or thought about taking a trip there? If so, where did (or would) you go? What are some of the reasons as to why you would choose these places?

_____

_____

_____

_____

_____

_____

Have you ever lived in or visited a place that is very cold in the winter? What are some winter activities you associate with extremely cold climates?

_____

_____

▶ Listening for the Gist 泛聽

Which cities do Wang Tao and Sun Xiaohua mention in this conversation?

		✓
Beijing	北京	
Nanjing	南京	
Shanghai	上海	
Chengdu	成都	
Guangdong	廣東	
Harbin	哈爾濱	
Xi'an	西安	

Which of them lived in northeastern China when young?

❑ 孫曉華   ❑ 王濤

▶ Listening for Details 靜聽

Which places in Beijing does Sun Xiaohua say she has visited?

			✓
Summer Palace	頤和園	Yíhéyuán	
Temple of Heaven	天壇	Tiāntán	
Confucian Temple	孔廟	Kǒngmiào	
Fragrant Hill Park	香山	Xiāngshān	

			✓
Great Wall	(萬里) 長城	Chángchéng	
Tian'an men Square	天安門	Tiān'ānmén	
Wang Fujing St.	王府井	Wángfǔjǐng	
Great Bell Temple	大鐘寺	Dàzhōngsì	
Palace Museum	故宮(博物館)	Gùgōng	
Beijing Zoo	動物園	Dòngwùyuán	
Beihai Park	北海公園	Běihǎigōngyuán	
Ming Tombs	(明)十三陵	Shísānlíng	

Wang Tao says "不到長城非好漢." One way to translate this expression is:

❑ Someone isn't a good Chinese if they haven't been to the Great Wall.

❑ If you don't go to the Great Wall you won't like China.

❑ If you don't go to the Great Wall you can't be good at Chinese.

Where in Beijing does Wang Tao's family live?

_____

Write down the most noteworthy thing mentioned about these places:

Xiangshan	
Wangfujing	
Chengdu	
Harbin	

Which of the speakers in this conversation likes to eat 麻辣火鍋?

❑ 孫曉華   ❑ 王濤

How cold does the temperature get in Harbin?

_____

Which of these words did Sun Xiaohua and Wang Tao use in this conversation when talking about the weather in different parts of China? (check all that apply)

	✓		✓
乾燥		涼快	
潮濕		冷	
熱		暖和	

Key Language Points 語言點

個/各 gè

It's easy to confuse 個 and 各 since both have the same pronunciation. Here are a few hints to keep in mind that will help you remember which one to use.

個 is often used as a non-specific measurement word.

個 is part of common words such as 個人 (individual), 個子 (stature, build) 個性 (gèxìng: personality or character).

各 often functions as a pronoun meaning "each" or "every" (e.g., 各有所好 hào each has his own likes [and dislikes]; 各有所長 cháng each has its strengths/strong points).

各 is also an adjective meaning "each" (e.g., 各式, 各方面, 各門課, 各位).

各 is also an adverb meaning "separately" or "differently."

Note the difference:

各個	N	each, every
	Adj	one by one, separately
個個	N	each and every one, all

Circle whether 各 or 個 is appropriate in the following sentences.

1. 孫曉華願意買　　個/各　　種好吃的東西。

2. 王濤的　　個/各　　子特別高。

3. 個/各　　人喜歡吃的火鍋不一樣。

4. 在王府井大街可以買　　個/各　　式　　個/各　　樣的小吃。

5. 每　　個/各　　人要參觀的地方不同。

6. 個/各　　位朋友，我們今天很高興，請大家乾杯。

7. 那　　個/各　　人的　　個/各　　性太強，很少有人要跟他去玩。

8. 個/各　　地人去王府井一定要吃糖葫蘆。

＊　＊　＊

Answer these questions according to the information given in this conversation and using the vocabulary item in parentheses.

1. 孫曉華願不願意住在一個很冷的地方？

_____（受不了）

2. 王濤小的時候喜歡玩什麼？玩得怎麼樣？

_____（根本）

＊　＊　＊

接著 + verb "to carry on, to continue"

Toward the end of this conversation, Sun Xiaohua said, "我們下次接著聊." How would you translate this statement?

_____

List three other verbs that could be used in this way:

接著＿＿＿＿＿＿＿

接著＿＿＿＿＿＿＿

接著＿＿＿＿＿＿＿

Follow-up Activities 應用

大家來説和寫 Role-Playing (Oral and Written)

With a partner, plan a trip to China. What are some of the places you want to see, and how many days do you want to spend in each place? Refer to a map of China and write out and discuss your itinerary. Be as detailed as possible.

大家來讀 Role-Playing (Reading)

Here is a seven-day itinerary suggested by a travel agent in Beijing and some close-up maps of the Great Wall at Badaling, Fragrant Mountain Park, and the Ming Tombs. Answer the following questions based on these materials.

游程安排

第一天　游天壇、北海。

第二天　游八達嶺長城、十三陵。

第三天　游香山、碧雲寺、頤和園。

第四天　早上乘游11次火車去承德，遊覽外八廟。

第五天　游避暑山莊，午後乘游12次返京。

第六天　游天安門、毛主席紀念堂、故宮、景山。

第七天　商業區購物。

交通工具

北京(火車)→承德(火車)→北京

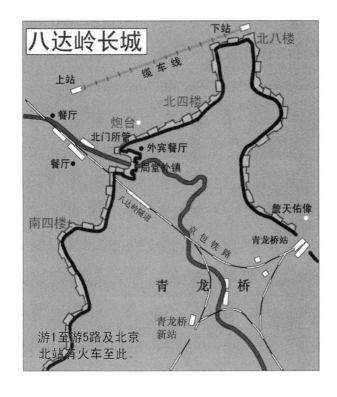

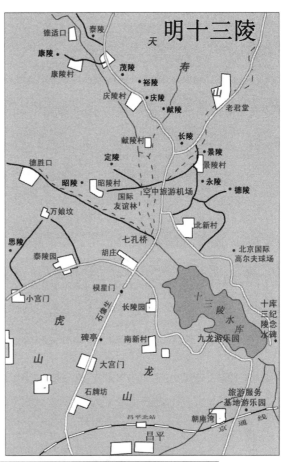

1. What other sight will be seen on the same day that you go to the Ming Tombs?

_____

2. Locate the Azure Dragon Bridge 青龍橋 at the Great Wall. What road is closest to it?

_____

3. What buses can you take to Fragrant Mountain Park?

_____

4. What three mountains are given on the map of the Ming Tombs?

_____

5. Which train will you take to Chengde 承德?

_____

6. Where in Fragrant Mountain Park is the Red Leaf Grove (紅葉林) located?

_____

7. How many restaurants are there at the Great Wall at Badaling? Can you find them all?

_____

8. What will you do on Day 7?

_____

Preparation 熱身

Rewrite the Chinese characters from the next page under the appropriate pictures.

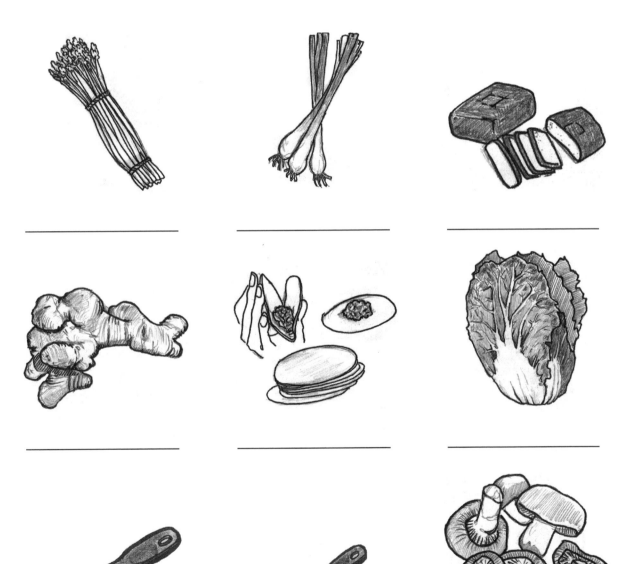

_____　　_____

豆腐　　　　　　　　大白菜　　　　　　　　餃子

餃子皮　　　　　　　韭菜　jiǔcài　　　　　湯匙　tāngchí

薑　jiāng　　　　　　茶匙　　　　　　　　磨菇　mógu (cf. 冬菇)

蔥　cōng　　　　　　豆(腐)乾　dòu(fǔ)gān

Do you know what each of these ingredients is? Write the English equivalent next to each item.
Here's a list from which to choose: salt, pepper, frying oil, sesame oil, wine, soy sauce, vinegar, sugar,
cornstarch, M.S.G.

Verbs + Objects

包餃子	baō jiǎozi	to wrap *jiaozi*
擀皮	gǎnpí	to make the wrapping (also called "skin")
和麵	huómiàn	to blend the flour, knead
拌餡	bànxiàn	to mix the stuffing (for the *jiaozi*)
調餡	tiáoxiàn	to mix the stuffing (for the *jiaozi*)

Additional Useful Vocabulary

去掉	qùdiào	V	to get rid of
緊	jǐn	Adj	tight, urgent
現成	xiànchéng	Adj	ready-made

As you will hear in this conversation, Wang Tao (Sun Xiaohua's friend) is a connoisseur of Chinese teas. Here is a list of some of his favorite varieties. Write the corresponding letter and number for the pīnyīn and English equivalent.

		pīnyīn	English
____ ____	龍井	a. júhuā	1. Jasmine
____ ____	烏龍	b. xiāng piàn	2. Chrysanthemum
____ ____	鐵觀音	c. lóngjǐng	3. Iron Guanyin
____ ____	香片	d. wūlóng	4. Dragon Well
____ ____	菊花	e. tiěguānyīn	5. Oolong

How many of these different types of tea have you tasted? Can you describe the flavor of each?

_____

_____

_____

_____

_____

▶ Listening for the Gist 泛聽

Why is Sun Xiaohua 孫曉華 so happy to see Wang Tao 王濤?

❑ She wants to ask him if he has any tea she could give her American friends.

❑ She wants to ask his advice about a dinner party she's planning.

❑ She wants to ask him to come to a dinner party.

❑ She wants to know where to buy ingredients for the food she is planning to cook at her dinner party.

Why is Sun Xiaohua worried? (check all that apply)

❑ She's not a very good cook.

❑ She's never entertained by herself before.

❑ She never made *jiaozi* before.

❑ She doesn't have a good recipe for *jiaozi*.

❑ She thinks her apartment is too small.

❑ She doesn't know how to wrap *jiaozi*.

❑ She doesn't know how to make the stuffing for *jiaozi*.

❑ She doesn't know if she'll be able to make everything in time.

▶ Listening for Details 靜聽

Based on the information given, complete this chart:

Date of dinner party	
Number of guests	
Time of dinner party	
Type of food they will eat	
Type of tea they will drink	
Nationality of dinner guests	

Which ingredients are used for the stuffing?

_____

How does Sun Xiaohua describe the *jiaozi* wrapping (餃子皮) she makes?

	✓
奇奇怪怪	
七手八腳	
奇形怪狀	
奇怪不像樣	
亂七八糟	

What does Wang Tao think she must be doing wrong? (answer in English)

_____

_____

According to Wang Tao, what is the biggest mistake people make when they prepare the stuffing?

_____

According to Wang Tao, what is the biggest mistake people make when they prepare the wrappers?

_____

Based on the conversation, indicate whether these statements are true 是 or false 非.

孫曉華跟王濤都是北方人。　　　　　　　　是　非

王濤願意幫孫曉華的忙。　　　　　　　　　是　非

王濤對做餃子非常有經驗。　　　　　　　　是　非

根據王濤的說法調餡的時候不能不放味精。　是　非

王濤說他會帶一些很好的龍井茶。　　　　　是　非

孫曉華的美國朋友沒喝過中國茶。　　　　　是　非

Key Language Points 語言點

verb 來 verb 去… "back and forth, over and over"

Toward the beginning of the conversation Sun Xiaohua said: "我想來想去,就覺得還是做餃子比較好." How would you translate her statement?

_____

Complete the phrases below by adding one of the following expressions. (Hint: you might need to add a little more context to some of the sentences.)

走來走去　　看來看去　　想來想去　　說來說去　　找來找去

Example:

孫曉華不知道她把王濤的電話號碼放在哪裡。

↳　孫曉華找來找去,可是找不到王濤的電話號碼。

1. 買菜的時候應該買什麼樣的肉。

2. 忘了怎麼翻譯 "龍井茶"。

_____

3. 不記得那個賣中國菜的商店在哪條路。

_____

4. 不懂菜譜寫的是什麼。 (càipǔ: cookbook)

_____

5. 沒告訴王濤她做過的餃子非常難吃。

_____

6. 書上沒有一個孫曉華不認識的字。

_____

Do you remember hearing these expressions in this conversation? If not, go back and listen again and see if you can figure out how they are used. Give a rough translation or paraphrase (in English) of the sentence or context in which these expressions occur.

取經

_____

_____

不怎麼在行

_____

_____

犯錯誤

_____

_____

所以說

_____

_____

Follow-up Activities 應用

大家來説 Role-Playing (Oral)

At the dinner party Sun Xiaohua's students talked about different kinds of Chinese food and tea that they had eaten and made before. With a partner enact one of these conversations. You might want to comment on some of the varieties of Chinese tea that Wang Tao brought for Sun Xiaohua's friends to try.

大家來寫 Role-Playing (Written)

Here is another recipe for *jiaozi*. Circle the ingredients that were not listed in Wang Tao's recipe.

豬肉 (絞 jiǎo: ground TW; 肉餡 PRC)	半斤*
韭菜(或大白菜半斤)	四兩
薑末	一茶匙
蔥花	一湯匙
醬油	一湯匙
酒	一茶匙

鹽   一茶匙

蔴油   二湯匙

花生油   一湯匙

水餃的餡，可按各人喜好採用牛肉、羊肉、雞肉或加入冬菇、
蝦仁、豆乾、磨菇、芹菜等。

*一斤＝十兩

According to the note given at the end of this list of ingredients, what else could be used instead of pork? (check all that apply)

	✓
shrimp	
lamb	
beef	
crabmeat	
turkey	
chicken	
fish	

What ingredients could be added? (check all that apply)

	✓
scallops	
shrimp	
beancurd	
carrots	
green beans	
mushrooms	
celery	
spinach	

Preparation 熱身

Useful Vocabulary

Draw a line matching the characters to the appropriate parts of the face.

眼睛			
耳朵			
眉毛			
鼻子			
嘴巴			
自從	zìcóng	Prep	since
哄	hǒng	V	to coax, to humor (children)
睏	kùn	Adj	想睡覺
抱	bào	V	to hold, to carry
餵	wèi	V	to feed (milk) (cf. 餵奶 to nurse)
尿布	niàobù	N	diapers
代價	dàijià	N	price, cost
體重	tǐzhòng	N	weight
身高	shēn'gāo	N	height
扶	fú	V	to support with hands, to hold onto
討人喜歡	tǎorén xǐhuan		likable (lit. "demands that one likes [him/her]")
爹	diē	N	父親, 爸爸

Here is a picture of Zhang Linsheng and his newborn daughter.

Imagine you are Zhang Linsheng and jot down what you might talk about if someone asked you what it's like to be a parent for the first time.

_____

_____

_____

_____

_____

_____

_____

▶ Listening for the Gist 泛聽

In this talk the father mentions… (check all that apply)

	✓
when the baby was born.	
what the baby is able to do.	
how the baby keeps the father busy.	

	✓
the financial cost of having a baby.	
how the baby pleases the father.	
his parents' reaction to having a granddaughter.	
the father's feelings about his baby.	
the sacrifices he has to make.	
a physical description of the baby.	

Check the word(s) that most appropriately fits the description of the father's feelings when he thinks of his daughter:

	✓		✓
tired		angry	
happy		loving	
bittersweet			

▶ Listening for Details 靜聽

Complete these sentences that the father uses to describe his emotional state:

苦得＿＿＿＿＿＿，樂得＿＿＿＿＿＿＿。

Ever since the baby was born, the father has not… (check all that apply)

	✓
gone to a movie.	
eaten a good meal.	
slept well.	
read a good book.	

In this monologue Zhang Linsheng uses the expression: 不當家不知柴米貴. The meaning of the saying is:

❑ You don't know how expensive rice and firewood are until you take charge of the cooking.

❑ You don't know how to cook unless you take charge of a family.

❏ You don't know how difficult it is to do something until you really do it.

❏ You don't know how costly things are until you have a child.

When the father says, "真沒想到當爸爸要付這麼大的代價," he means:

	✓
It is so expensive to buy clothing for his daughter.	
It is so costly to have a baby.	
The price of having children is too great to imagine.	
The price of being a father is really high.	

In what order does the father talk about the way his daughter looks?

鼻子	
眼睛	
眉毛	
嘴巴	
舌頭	
頭髮	

The baby was taken to a doctor to have a health check. Please fill out the following chart:

姓名：	性別：	年齡：
身高：　　　英寸	體重：　　　磅	換尿布：　次／天
能力：他（她）會不會做以下動作		
☐ 微笑	☐ 大笑	
☐ 説話	☐ "唱歌"	
☐ 坐	☐ 站	
☐ 爬	☐ 走	
☐ 吃固體食物	☐ 翻身	

Key Language Points 語言點

Imagine you are a father. If your child were to do the following, what would you do? (Use Chinese characters or pīnyīn.) The first one has been done for you.

如果小孩…	爸爸要…
累了	要哄
餓了	＿＿＿＿＿
哭了	＿＿＿＿＿
醒了	＿＿＿＿＿
咳嗽了	＿＿＿＿＿
尿布濕了	＿＿＿＿＿
冷了	＿＿＿＿＿
渴了	＿＿＿＿＿
睏了	＿＿＿＿＿
發燒了	＿＿＿＿＿

＊　＊　＊

Respond to the following statements or questions based on what you think Zhang Linsheng might say. Be sure to use the patterns indicated in parentheses.

1. 當爸爸有什麼苦？(光是…就)

2. 你女兒才四個月就會站了。是真的嗎？(沒想到)

_____

3. 既然當父親這麼苦，你就別當父親了。(再 + verb)

_____

Follow-up Activities 應用

大家來說 Role-Playing (Oral)

Here are two pictures of Zhang Linsheng and his daughter. With a partner, discuss how she has changed from the first picture to the next, and what changes you imagine have occurred in her relationship with her father.

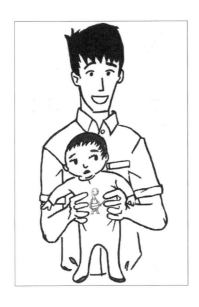 

大家來寫 **Role-Playing (Written)**

Write out a telephone conversation between you and your parents about the reason(s) why you want or don't want to have children. Be sure that each speaker has at least 10–15 substantial lines of dialogue.

_____

_____

_____

_____

_____

_____

_____

_____

_____

_____

_____

_____

_____

_____

Preparation 熱身

Useful Vocabulary

引起	yǐnqǐ	V	to cause
評論	pínglùn	V	to comment on, to discuss
		N	commentary, critique, review
榮幸	róngxìng	N	honor
評論家	pínglùnjiā	N	critic, reviewer
預料	yùliào	V	to expect, to predict
具體	jùtǐ	Adv	concretely, specifically
吵架	chǎojià	V	to argue
慘	cǎn	Adj	tragic, miserable, disastrous
意外	yìwài	Adj	unexpected
行爲	xíngwéi	N	behavior, conduct
尋找	xúnzhǎo	V	to seek
光明	guāngmíng	N	light
敏感	mǐn'gǎn	Adj	sensitive
異性	yìxìng	N	opposite sex
允許	yǔnxǔ	V	to allow
衝突	chōngtū	N	conflict
根源	gēnyuán	N	root, origin, basis

What are five things that you expect to hear in a news story about a celebrity murder case? (Write in Chinese or English.)

_____

_____

_____

_____

_____

_____

_____

▶ Listening for the Gist 泛聽

Who is Gu Cheng 顧城?

	✓
a movie star	
an athlete	
a poet	
a singer	
a politician	

Whom did he kill?

	✓
his best friend	
his agent	
his girlfriend	
his wife	
his wife's lover	

Who is being interviewed? (check all that apply)

	✓
a literary critic	
a reporter	
Gu Cheng's lover	
Gu Cheng's friend	
a detective	
an actress	
a good friend of Gu Cheng's wife	

▶ Listening for Details 靜聽

The island Gu Cheng lived on is off the coast of…

	✓
Hainan	
Taiwan	
New Zealand	
Hawaii	

According to Ms. Chen, Gu Cheng had recently enjoyed what activities? (check all that apply)

	✓
fishing	
writing	
planting a garden	
getting together with friends	
designing a website	

Indicate whether the following statements are true (是) or false (非).

Ms. Chen hadn't talked to Gu Cheng in a long time.	是	非
Ms. Chen knew the news Thursday night.	是	非
Gu Cheng's older sister was at the scene of the crime.	是	非
Gu Cheng killed his wife with a knife.	是	非
Gu Cheng also killed himself.	是	非
Ms. Chen had no idea why Gu Cheng would act in this way.	是	非

Listening to the interview, complete the lines of the poem Ms. Chen quoted. How would you translate these lines?

黑夜＿＿＿＿＿＿＿＿＿＿＿＿＿＿＿＿眼睛；

＿＿＿＿＿＿＿＿＿＿＿＿＿＿＿尋找光明。

＿＿＿＿＿＿＿＿＿＿＿＿＿＿＿＿＿＿＿＿＿＿＿＿＿＿＿＿＿＿＿＿＿

＿＿＿＿＿＿＿＿＿＿＿＿＿＿＿＿＿＿＿＿＿＿＿＿＿＿＿＿＿＿＿＿＿

＿＿＿＿＿＿＿＿＿＿＿＿＿＿＿＿＿＿＿＿＿＿＿＿＿＿＿＿＿＿＿＿＿

What does Ms. Chen say about this couplet? Do you agree? Why? Why not?

＿＿＿＿＿＿＿＿＿＿＿＿＿＿＿＿＿＿＿＿＿＿＿＿＿＿＿＿＿＿＿＿＿

＿＿＿＿＿＿＿＿＿＿＿＿＿＿＿＿＿＿＿＿＿＿＿＿＿＿＿＿＿＿＿＿＿

＿＿＿＿＿＿＿＿＿＿＿＿＿＿＿＿＿＿＿＿＿＿＿＿＿＿＿＿＿＿＿＿＿

Put the radio announcer's comments in the order in which they were spoken during this interview.

＿＿＿＿今天我們節目的時間到了。

＿＿＿＿你能不能告訴我們當時的具體的情況呢？

＿＿＿＿我們再一次向陳小姐表示感謝。

＿＿＿今天我們榮幸地請到了著名評論家也是顧城的生前好友陳穎女士。

＿＿＿聽說當時的情況非常慘。

＿＿＿這也是悲劇的根源。

＿＿＿大概沒有一個人會預料會有這樣的事情發生。

按照陳小姐的說法，顧城跟他太太為什麼吵架？

_____

_____

Key Language Points 語言點

Write the letter of the synonym or definition from Column B that corresponds to each expression in Column A.

Column A	Column B
＿＿＿ 如意	a. 太太
＿＿＿ 著名	b. 讓
＿＿＿ 意外	c. 吵架
＿＿＿ 死去	d. 不會達到某種程度
＿＿＿ 口角	e. 沒想到
＿＿＿ 預料	f. 行為
＿＿＿ 允許	g. 事前推測
＿＿＿ 不至於	h. 有名
＿＿＿ 妻子	i. 去世
	j. 達到自己的願望

＊　＊　＊

Which of these expressions were used in this interview in reference to Gu Cheng? (circle all that apply)

震驚	奇怪	敏感	瘋了一樣
悲傷	如意	生氣	崇高的感情
衝動	漂亮	聰明	愛所有的異性
嫉妒	著名	不高興	

How would you translate Ms. Chen's comment: 我不在場?

	✓
I wasn't on the scene.	
I'm not in that field.	
I'm not part of that group (of his friends).	

＊　＊　＊

Match the verbs to the objects that occurred with them in this interview. (**Note:** some verbs are used more than once.)

引起	光明
發生	意外
感到	消息
聽到	評論
發表	慘劇
尋找	生命
	轟動

Follow-up Activities 應用

大家來説 Role-Playing (Oral)

In a similar case, a woman named Song Yuying was arrested for killing her husband and his mistress. You and your partner are the defense lawyer and prosecutor. You are arguing the case in court.

大家來寫 Role-Playing (Written)

Later Ms. Chen thought of another poem written by Gu Cheng. How would you read this poem in light of the comments given by Ms. Chen in this interview? See if you can translate it into English and then write a short paragraph in Chinese explaining how you interpret it.

感覺　　　　　　　　　_____

天是灰色的　　　　　_____

路是灰色的　　　　　_____

樓是灰色的　　　　　_____

雨是灰色的　　　　　_____

在一片死灰中　　　　_____

走過兩個孩子　　　　_____

一個鮮紅　　　　　　_____

一個淡綠　　　　　　_____

Preparation 熱身

Useful Vocabulary

文言文	wényánwén	N	Classical Chinese
理論	lǐlùn	N	theory
古典文學/ 現代文學	gǔdiǎn wénxué/ xiàndài wénxué	N	Classical/Modern literature
方式	fāngshì	N	way, style
角度	jiǎodù	N	angle, perspective
觀點	guāndiǎn	N	point of view, standpoint
態度	tàidù	N	attitude, approach
交流	jiāoliú	V	to exchange
碩士	shuòshì	N	Master's Degree
博士	bóshì	N	Ph.D.
論文	lùnwén	N	thesis
尤其(是)	yóuqí (shì)	Adv	especially
虛字	xūzì	N	particles
掌握	zhǎngwò	V	to grasp
之乎者也	zhīhūzhěyě	Ph	four classical particles that are used as a phrase to indicate pedantic language

How many of these Chinese dynasties (cháodài 朝代) have you heard of? Jot down below what (if anything) you know about them or about premodern Chinese literature.

			✓
Zhōu	周	11th century–256 B.C.E.	
Qín	秦	221–207 B.C.E.	
Hàn	漢	206 B.C.E.–C.E. 220	
Táng	唐	618–907	
Sòng	宋	960–1279	
Yúan	元	1271–1368	
Míng	明	1368–1644	
Qīng	清	1644–1911	

_____

_____

_____

_____

_____

_____

_____

▶ Listening for the Gist 泛聽

方萍是什麼樣的學生?   幾年級?

   ❑ 大學生   ❑ 一   ❑ 二

   ❑ 研究生   ❑ 三   ❑ 四

Check which of these topics were mentioned in this conversation.

	✓
Differences in teaching methods in China and the U.S.	
Differences in classroom dynamics in China and the U.S.	
Specific areas of Chinese literature Fang Ping is studying	
Fang Ping's favorite topics in Chinese literature	
Why American students study Classical Chinese	
The number of students in the class she helps teach	
The materials students are reading in Classical Chinese	
Wang Tao's opinion about studying Classical Chinese	

▶ Listening for Details 靜聽

What is Fang Ping going to do when she runs into Wang Tao?

- ❑ Go to the library to check out some materials
- ❑ Go to the library to return a book
- ❑ Go home to study
- ❑ Go home to grade papers
- ❑ Teach Classical Chinese
- ❑ Meet with students from her Classical Chinese class

What does Fang Ping think is different about studying traditional Chinese literature in the U.S. versus studying it in China? (answer in English)

_____

_____

Match the type of literature that Fang Ping has studied with the dynasty that she mentions:

詩 shī   poetry   漢

詞 cí   lyrics   元

賦 fù   rhapsody   唐

宋

她寫碩士論文的時候可能會選什麼題目？

	✓
漢代的賦	
唐代的賦	
唐代的詩	
唐代的詞	
宋代的詩	
宋代的詞	
元代的詞	
清代的詩	

Complete this chart:

Topic of the course Fang Ping is teaching	
Number of students in her class	
Other Chinese courses students are taking	
Are the students Chinese majors?	
How long the course has been in session	
What the students have learned so far	

What is Wang Tao's reaction when he hears that there are many American students studying Classical Chinese? Why?

_____

_____

Key Language Points 語言點

交流 jiāoliú   交換 jiāohuàn

Both these terms are verbs that mean "to exchange," but they are not interchangeable. 交換 usually refers to a more limited, one-time exchange or a swap whereas 交流 expresses an ongoing process, usually involving abstract nouns such as ideas, experiences, or viewpoints. Which of these terms does Wang Ping use in conversation? Do you remember what she says? Write her sentence down here.

_____

Complete the following sentences using either 交流 or 交換 depending on the context.

1. 聖誕節的時候有的人喜歡_____禮物。

2. 王濤今年是中國的_____學生。

3. 方萍願意跟別的學生_____經驗。

4. 這兩個大學在教學上互相_____。

5. 方萍覺得他跟他的美國同學可以做思想上的_____。

＊　＊　＊

到⋯為止 **"up to, as far as"**

到 date or time expression 為止

到 a condition is met or a situation reached a certain result 為止

What does Fang Ping say has happened 到現在為止?

_____

Translate the sentences below that also use this construction:

1. 到現在為止，王濤還沒有很多機會跟美國學生來往。

_____

_____

2. 方萍昨天晚上在圖書館翻譯漢賦。雖然她已經很累了，但她還堅持 (jiānchí: persist in, insist on) 到把整篇漢賦翻完為止。

_____

_____

3. 到目前為止，中文系的學生對學文言文一直很感興趣。

_____

_____

* * *

可 + verb = verb + able, can be verbed

Both Fang Ping and Wang Tao agree that the number of students in Fang Ping's classical Chinese course is a 可觀的數目 (kěguānde shùmù: considerable or impressive number). Notice how adding the word kě before a verb turns that verb into an adjective (or stative verb), showing the potential mood (i.e., something can or is able to have that quality).

How would you translate these terms that consist of 可 + a verb? See if you can figure them out without looking at a dictionary.

可笑 _____ 可愛 _____ 可怕 _____

可口 _____ 可恨 hèn _____ 可憐 lián _____

可靠 kào _____   可信 _____   可見 _____

可恥 chǐ _____   可惜 xī _____   可貴 _____

Follow-up Activities 應用

大家來寫 **Role-Playing (Written)**

Wang Tao decided to take Fang Ping up on her offer and visit her Classical Chinese course. He was quite surprised to discover that students were readings passages from *Lunyu* (the *Analects*) and were carefully learning the grammar of every line they read. After the class he decided to write an article about this group of American students learning Classical Chinese. He wanted to conduct the interview completely in Chinese. Help him think of five questions he could ask them and three questions he could ask the instructors. Write down the questions below.

Questions for the students:

1. _____

_____

2. _____

_____

3. _____

_____

4. _____

_____

5. _____

_____

Questions for the instructors:

1. _____

   _____

2. _____

   _____

3. _____

   _____

大家來説 **Role-Playing (Oral)**

Using these questions, interview two or three students (in Chinese) who you know who are now studying Classical Chinese. Also, if possible, interview the instructor.

Now prepare a brief oral presentation on this topic, based on your interviews and based on the conversation between Wang Tao and Fang Ping.

_____

_____

_____

_____

_____

_____

_____

_____

Preparation 熱身

Useful Vocabulary

奮鬥	fèndòu	V	to struggle
歡樂	huānlè	Adj	很高興
移民	yímín	N	immigrant
破破爛爛	pòpòlànlàn	Adj	dilapidated, shabby
掙錢	zhèngqián	VO	賺錢
豪富	háofù	Adj	powerful and wealthy
大哥大	dàgēdà	N	cell phone (cf. 行動電話)
妙	miào	Adj	1. excellent, fine; 2. subtle, clever
空虛	kōngxū	Adj	void, emptiness, 沒有意義
孤單	gūdān	Adj	alone, 沒有朋友
轟動	hōngdòng	V	to cause a sensation, to make a stir
矛盾	máodùn	N	contradiction; contradictory
遙遠	yáoyuǎn	Adj	distant, remote
陌生	mòshēng	Adj	unfamiliar
恐懼	kǒngjù	N	fear, dread
冷淡	lěngdàn	Adj	cold, indifferent

What is a film you recently saw that has something to do with China or with Chinese people? Jot down the main plot and key characters and whether it involves universal themes such as issues of personal identity, family, or generational conflicts, etc. With a partner, discuss this film and its significance in Chinese.

_____

_____

_____

_____

_____

▶ Listening for the Gist 泛聽

The people talking in this conversation are…

❑ two friends

❑ a reporter and a writer

❑ a television critic and an actor

Which of the speakers has seen this television series?

	✓
the male speaker	
the female speaker	
both speakers	

This program they are discussing is about a…

	✓
New Yorker in Beijing.	
man from Beijing now living in New York.	
New Yorker who visited Beijing and returns to New York.	
man from Beijing who visited New York and returns to Beijing.	

Mr. Wang, the main character,…

	✓
is very poor.	
is very rich.	
starts out very poor and becomes wealthy.	
starts out wealthy and becomes very poor.	

In the television show Mr. Wang has a… (check all that apply)

	✓
wife	
son	
father	
daughter	
mother	
niece	

Where was this program originally shown on television?

_____

The TV show is very popular because people… (check all that apply)

	✓
like the main character (Mr. Wang).	
want to know about life in America.	
want to immigrate to the U.S. and become wealthy.	
want to know about the Chinese-American way of life.	
enjoy making fun of life in America.	

▶ Listening for Details 靜聽

Indicate whether the following statements are true (是) or false (非):

When Mr. Wang first arrives in New York, he...

speaks English very well.	是	非
has to do the hardest job.	是	非
has little money.	是	非
doesn't understand U.S. society very well.	是	非
has a friend who helps him considerably.	是	非

Check all of Mr. Wang's experiences that are mentioned in this discussion of 北京人在紐約.

	✓
His successes	
His happiness	
His guilt	
His suffering	
His misfortunes	
His good luck	
When he made money	
When his parents died	
His marriage	
His divorce	
His failures	

When Mr. Wang first arrived in New York, what are some of the problems he faced?

	✓
他身體不好	
他不太會說英語	
他沒有什麼錢	
他太太離開了他	
他父母要他回中國去	

Complete the following sentences that describe what he did during those difficult times.

1. 他住在一個_____

2. 他去中國餐館幹最_____

3. 他常常被_____

The woman in this conversation says 深有同感. Do you think this comment is one of:

	✓
pity?	
empathy?	
ridicule?	
irony?	

How would you translate it?

_____

What are some of the ways Mr. Wang later demonstrated his success?

	✓
He bought an expensive car.	
He rented a huge apartment in Manhattan.	
He wore imported clothing.	
He owned a fancy house.	
He used a cell phone.	
He owned a state-of-the-art computer system.	
He entertained lavishly.	
He ran his own company.	

＊　＊　＊

Which of the following statement(s) would Mr. Wang probably disagree with? (NOTE: there may be more than one correct answer.)

1. 錢不能給一個人歡樂。

4. 錢不能解決任何問題。

2. 有錢的人一定不幸福。

5. 有很多錢不見得是一件好事。

3. 就是你有錢，你也可能會有別的問題。

Key Language Points 語言點

Write the letter of the word from Column B that is the closest antonym to each word in Column A.

Column A	Column B
_____ 陌生	a. 倒楣(霉)
_____ 成功	b. 充實
_____ 走運	c. 地獄
_____ 痛苦	d. 失敗
_____ 天堂	e. 熟悉
_____ 冷淡	f. 失望
_____ 空虛	g. 歡樂
	h. 熱情

Write the letter of the word from Column B that is the closest synonym to each word in Column A.

Column A	Column B
_____ 欺負	a. 轟動
_____ 恐懼	b. 寂寞
_____ 發財	c. 幹活
_____ 孤單	d. 好
_____ 一切	e. 怕
_____ 打工	f. 大錢
_____ 妙	g. 被別人騙
	h. 所有的

In the dialogue, the male speaker says: 他既沒有錢，又不會說英語. What other sentence pattern beside 既…又… could be used in this sentence that would express a similar meaning?

_____

_____

Follow-up Activities 應用

大家來寫和說 Role-Playing (Written & Oral)

Imagine an interview between a TV reporter and the actor who plays the role of Mr. Wang in this series. First write five to eight thought-provoking questions that you would ask (in Chinese, of course). Then interview a classmate who is willing to play the part of Mr. Wang. If you run out of things to talk about regarding this particular TV show, imagine that this actor recently played a leading role in a Chinese film that you both have seen.

1. _____

2. _____

3. _____

4. _____

5. _____

6. _____

7. _____

8. _____

Lesson 42　第四十二課

Interviewing a Physically Disabled Student 訪問殘疾學生

Preparation 熱身

Useful Vocabulary

殘疾	cánjí	N	disability
設施	shèshī	N	facilities
輪椅	lúnyǐ	N	wheelchair
通道	tōngdào	N	ramp
限制	xiànzhì	N	limitations, restrictions
障礙	zhàng'ài	N	obstacle
差異	chāyì	N	difference, discrepancy
缺陷	quēxiàn	N	shortcoming, flaw
激烈	jīliè	Adj	fierce, intense
技能	jìnéng	N	technical ability, mastery of a skill
草擬	cǎonǐ	V	to draft, to draw up

You are going to hear an interview with a student from China who has had polio since childhood. Jot down five concerns you think she might have about living and studying in the U.S.

_____

_____

_____

_____

_____

▶ Listening for the Gist 泛聽

Which of these issues were mentioned in the interview?

	✓		✓
transportation		financial losses	
education		personal struggle	
employment		physical therapy	
marriage		public facilities	
legal issues		daily life	

How would you describe the attitude of the woman being interviewed? What gives you this impression? (answer in English)

_____

_____

_____

What is your impression of the radio announcer? Why? (answer in English)

_____

_____

_____

▶ Listening for Details 靜聽

The name of the woman being interviewed is...

	✓
Wang Xiaoyin	
Huang Xiaoyin	
Wang Xiaoyan	
Wang Xiaoying	
Huang Xiaoying	

How long has she been in the U.S.?

	✓
More than one month	
More than two months	
More than three months	
Over half a year	
A year	
A few weeks	

中國現在的殘疾人有多少?

	✓
500,000	
5,000,000	
50,000,000	
500,000,000	

為了解決在外面上廁所的困難, 有的殘疾人⋯

	✓
穿上成人用的尿布	
先吃一點藥	
出門之前不喝水	
整天呆在家裡	

小英提到, 在中國進入大學之前要經過

	✓
老師介紹	
身體檢查	
學科考試	
政治審查	

大部分在中國的殘疾人只能做的工作是

	看門	打字	教學	聽電話	做衣服	收報紙
✓						

小英來美國念的是

	大學一年級	大學四年級	碩士學位	博士學位
✓				

節目主持人說小英是"自學成才"。小英自學的是

	外語	圖書館學	新聞學	電子工程
✓				

In which country does Xiaoying find these problems more serious?

	中國	美國
沒有殘疾人洗手間		
沒有家人的照顧		
沒有輪椅通道		
沒有免費醫療		
沒有大學接受她		
沒有圖書館和宿舍		

What does Xiaoying say she intends to tell her friends with disabilities back in China?

_____

_____

_____

Key Language Points 語言點

Do you remember the meaning of each of these compounds with 專 zhuān? See if you can translate each below. Which of these compounds with 專 did you hear in this conversation? Circle each term.

專業 _____   專用 _____   專門 _____

專心 _____   專家 _____   專長 _____

* * *

Which of these expressions can be used to introduce examples or offer clarification?

譬如 pìrú   看樣子   例如 lìrú   舉例來説   對於

比如   另一方面   像   這樣   比方説   就是説

* * *

相當(於)　V　　to correspond to, to be equal to (cf. 等於, 跟…一樣)
　　　　　Adj　suitable, appropriate
　　　　　Adv　considerably, quite

In this interview the host of the radio show (節目主持人) and Xiaoying both use the term 相當 several times. Circle who said which of these comments.

相當的不簡單！　　　　　　　　　節目主持人　　小英
拿到了相當於大學畢業的文憑。　　節目主持人　　小英
那相當好。　　　　　　　　　　　節目主持人　　小英

Now rewrite each of the following sentences using 相當.

1. 小英認為她有非常多機會。

2. 她總是覺得她挺幸運。

_____

3. 按照她老師的說法，在高中學三年的英文跟在大學學一年的英文一樣。

_____

_____

4. 在中國很多殘疾人找不到合適的工作。

_____

＊　＊　＊

Write the letter of the synonym or definition from Column B that corresponds to each expression in Column A.

Column A	Column B
_____ 必須	a. 生活上的問題多
_____ 發揮 fāhuī	b. 不收錢
_____ 就業	c. 行動
_____ 困難	d. 分別
_____ 摁　　èn	e. 不方便
_____ 審查 shěnchá	f. 把內在的能力表現出來
_____ 免費 miǎnfèi	g. 用手按
_____ 不便	h. 得到工作
_____ 差異	i. 一定要
	j. 仔細檢查

＊　＊　＊

Write the letter of the antonym from Column B that corresponds to each expression in Column A.

Column A	Column B
_____ 減少 jiǎnshǎo	a. 倒楣
_____ 安全	b. 長處
_____ 幸運 xìngyùn	c. 難過
_____ 缺陷	d. 危險
_____ 愉快 yúkuài	e. 增加
	f. 快樂

Follow-up Activities 應用

大家來說 Role-Playing (Oral)

Later that month Xiaoying was planning to travel from Denver to Richmond, Virginia to visit some friends who live there. She will need to change planes either in Washington D.C. or Chicago. She has decided to talk to the customer-assistance specialist at O'Hare International Airport and the one at Dulles International Airport to find out about how she'll be able to manage her luggage and transfer to the second flight and how long a layover there will be between flights. She's also concerned about the facilities available at each airport, especially if she needs to eat a meal or buy some gifts for her friends. Help her enact these phone conversations so she can make the best decision.

大家來讀 Role-Playing (Reading)

Recently the Chinese government sent out a survey (調查 diàochá) to all physically disabled students. Please help Xiaoying complete this form. First answer some short questions that will give you some helpful hints about some of the vocabulary in the survey that may be unfamiliar.

1. A translation of the heading of this survey is:

_____

2. In this questionnaire, what do the instructions 可選擇多項 mean?

❏ You can choose multiple items.

❏ There are many choices for disabled people.

❏ Disabled people are often allowed to choose many topics.

3. 建築 jiànzhù (jiànzhú) as a verb means "to construct, to build." As a noun it means "construction, building, structure." It also means "architecture." What do you think 建築物 means in this context?

Now you are ready to complete the questionnaire according to the information you heard in the interview.

關於殘疾人保障法的調查

姓名：＿＿＿＿＿＿＿＿　　性別：　　男　　女

年齡：　　21-35　　　　36-50　　　　50以上

工作單位：＿＿＿＿＿＿＿＿＿＿＿

教育程度：☐ 小學畢業　☐ 初中畢業　☐ 高中畢業

☐ 中專畢業　☐ 大專畢業

☐ 大學畢業或同等學歷

我國政府正在草擬殘疾人保障法，請你提意見。

一、殘疾人的權利應在哪些方面得到保障？（可選擇多項）

☐ 受高等教育的機會　　☐ 就業機會

☐ 房屋分配　　☐ 交通服務

二、你認為新的建築物應該規定有哪些設施？

☐ 殘疾人保健室　　☐ 自動售貨機　　☐ 遙控門*

☐ 殘疾人洗手間　　☐ 自動門　　☐ 輪椅通道

☐ 小型摩托車**專用道　　☐ 電暖爐　　☐ 電梯

謝謝！

---

* remote control gate　　　　** scooter

大家來寫 **Role-Playing (Written)**

After this interview Xiao Ying wrote a letter to a close friend in China who is also physically disabled. In this letter she wrote about her current experience as a student in the U.S. Be sure to mention specific differences between handicapped students in the U.S. and in China, and also her interactions with American students. (This letter should be 80–120 Chinese characters long).

_____

_____

_____

_____

_____

_____

_____

_____

_____

_____

_____

_____

_____

_____

_____

_____

Preparation 熱身

Useful Vocabulary

陸續	lùxù	Adv	in succession, one after another (陸陸續續地)
衝擊	chōngjǐ	N	clash, conflict
如何	rúhé	Adv	how (cf. 怎麼)
取捨	qǔshě	V	to accept or reject, to make one's choice
綜合	zōnghé	V	to synthesize, to blend
傳授	chuánshòu	V	to pass on, to teach, to impart
以...為榮	yǐ ... wéiróng		to take X as an honor
嚴格	yángé	Adj	strict, rigorous
灌輸	guànshū	V	to teach, to imbue with, to instill
血統	xuètóng	N	blood relationship, lineage
(考試)卷子	juànzi	N	test paper
生成	shēngchéng	V	to be born
幼兒所*	yòu'ér suǒ	N	kindergarten (*Ms. Li meant to say 托兒所 tuō'ér suǒ; cf. 幼稚園 TW; 幼兒園 PRC)

A Chinese friend of yours is describing to you her experience of raising her children in America. Think about the types of conflicts that parents might face when their children grow up in a culture different from the one in which they grew up. Jot down five examples.

_____

_____

_____

_____

_____

_____

_____

▶ Listening for the Gist 泛聽

Of the following topics, check all that you heard the speaker talk about:

	✓
Her name	
Her background	
How long she has been in the U.S.	
Names of her children	
Her goals in raising her children	
Chinese popular music	
American popular music	
Studying Chinese language	
Her children's friends	
Listening to the radio	
Advice she gives her children	
Difficulties her children face in being both Chinese and American	

How many Chinese sayings does she quote toward the end of her comments?

一   二   三   四

▶ Listening for Details 靜聽

Complete this chart based on what you heard in this monologue.

Her name (give pīnyīn)	
Number of children	
Ages of children (specify which one[s])	
How long she has been in the U.S.	
Where she is from	
Grades her children are in	

Select the phrase that best completes each of the following sentences based on what the speaker said.

她三個孩子一定要…

	✓
學會如何說中文，看中文，寫中文。	
每天吃中國菜，也要學會怎麼做中國菜。	
將來住在臺灣。	
多交一些中國朋友。	

她跟她老大開車去…

	✓
超級市場	
中文學校	
朋友家	
購物中心	

她說西方的社會⋯

	✓
是不容易了解的。	
比較注重自我。	
比較注重錢。	
不太注重教育。	

她覺得最大的難題是⋯

	✓
不知道應該用什麼方法教育孩子。	
強迫孩子學中文。	
孩子們對中國社會沒有興趣。	
如何勸孩子跟中國人結婚。	

她的兒子為什麼把收音機關掉了？ (請用中文回答)

Ms. Li refers to a couple of frequently used Chinese sayings toward the end of her monologue. The first is: 覆巢之下無完卵 fú cháo zhī xià wú wán luǎn (覆巢無完卵), which literally means "if the nest is overturned there won't be any whole eggs left." Which of the following are extended meanings of this expression? (check all that apply)

❑ In a total disaster no one will survive.

❑ If a country is defeated, all its people will suffer.

❑ If chaos occurs, only the strong will survive.

❑ Sometimes it's better to abandon a sinking ship.

❑ People with experience will be needed in times of trouble.

How does it relate to what she's talking about here?

The second saying she mentions is: "我走過的橋比你吃的飯還要多."
Unfortunately she actually confused two different sayings, which are: (1) "我走過的橋比你走過的路還要多" and (2) "我吃過的鹽比你吃的飯還要多."
How would you translate these sayings?

1. _____

2. _____

How do you think you might react if your parents or someone older than you said one or both of these phrases to you? Why?

_____

Key Language Points 語言點

Match each word in Column A with the word or phrase with the same or similar meaning in Column B.

Column A	Column B
_____ 缺點	a. 嚴格
_____ 傳授	b. 長處
_____ 難題	c. 不知道
_____ 取捨	d. 不容易解決的問題
_____ 收音機	e. 把技藝教給別人
_____ 優點	f. 短處
_____ 不曉得	g. 要或不要
	h. 聽廣播的機器

＊　＊　＊

Below is a paragraph Ms. Li wrote in a letter to a friend once when she was thinking about this same topic. Fill in the blanks with words from the following list. Not all the words will be used.

傳授	文化	陸續
了解	比較	教育
自我	交	感受
差異	嚴格	傳統

我從小受的是中國的＿＿＿＿＿＿。但是我孩子所接觸的＿＿＿＿＿＿完全是西方的，＿＿＿＿＿＿的也都是西方的朋友。我覺得西方社會＿＿＿＿＿＿注重＿＿＿＿＿＿，而中國人會更多地想到別人需要或＿＿＿＿＿＿。我希望我的孩子多＿＿＿＿＿＿中國文化和西方文化在這方面的＿＿＿＿＿＿。

Follow-up Activities 應用

大家來說 Role-Playing (Oral)

Find a partner and talk about the times when your parents embarrassed you. Did these events mainly occur because of cultural differences between you and your parents or because of generational differences? Be sure to give specific examples.

大家來寫 Role-Playing (Written)

Imagine that you are this woman's son or daughter. Write a letter to a friend explaining how you feel about growing up as a Chinese American. Try to include the following vocabulary:

態度　嚴格　優點　觀念　教育　要求　以…為榮　注重 傳統　綜合

Preparation 熱身

Useful Vocabulary

圓桌	yuán zhuō	N	round (shaped) table
共享	gòngxiǎng	V	to share, to enjoy together
土生土長	tǔshēng tǔzhǎng	Ph	locally born and bred
融合	rónghé	V	to mix together, to blend
同樣	tóngyàng	Adv	equally, similarly
(不)僅僅	bùjǐnjǐn	Adv	(not) merely, (not) only
期望	qíwàng, qīwàng	N	希望
苛責	kēzé	V	to criticize severely
多餘	duōyú	Adj	excessive, uncalled for, unnecessary
鼓勵	gǔlì	V	to encourage
鋪床	pūchuáng	V O	to make a bed
蓋(一個)章	gài (yīgè) zhāng	V O	to affix a stamp
及格	jígé	V	to pass a test (不及格, to fail a test)
自信心	zìxìnxīn	N	self-confidence
自尊心	zìzūnxīn	N	self-esteem

▶ Listening for the Gist 泛聽

Which of these topics does the speaker mention in this talk?

	✓
Why she went to Taiwan	
Where she stayed	
Ages of her children	
Her children's table manners	
Table manners of people who live in Taiwan	
Expectations of teachers in the U.S.	
Expectations of teachers in Taiwan	
Expectations of Chinese parents	
Expectations of American parents	
Chinese students' sense of responsibility	
American students' sense of responsibility	
Her hopes for her children	
Her hopes for herself	

▶ Listening for Details 靜聽

Complete this chart based on what you heard in this monologue:

How long did Ms. Li stay in Taiwan?	
How many children did she bring with her?	
What did they do?	
Where did they live?	
Why did she take her children there?	
What gender are her children?	
What are the ages of her children?	

Explain some of the cultural differences Ms. Li mentioned in these situations (write your answers in English):

Eating at a friend's home	
Eating *jiaozi* at a restaurant	
Taking a spelling test in the U.S.	

What does Ms. Li mean when she says that Chinese people often "觀察別人的臉色"? Do you think Americans do this too?

_____

What were some of Li Yinghui's responsibilities when she was a student? (check all that apply)

❑ Make her bed.

❑ Clean her room.

❑ Help cook dinner.

❑ Do well in her schoolwork.

Answer the following questions in Chinese.

1. 根據李小姐的説法，中國人吃飯的時候為什麼不會把菜吃光？

_____

_____

2. 她為什麼覺得，剛來美國的時候，自己這麼不能幹？

_____

_____

3. 李小姐認為美國的孩子養成了什麼壞習慣？

_____

_____

Key Language Points 語言點

主義

What does the speaker of this monologue say about 自我主義? Write down the context in which she uses this term.

_____

The suffix 主義 zhǔyì means "theory" or "doctrine" and is added to many words to mean "-ism," as in 自我主義, egoism.

Match the following terms:

馬克思主義	Impressionism
社會主義	Feminism
資本主義	Anarchism
國際主義	Fatalism
共產主義	Socialism
印象主義	Individualism
女權主義	Capitalism
民族主義	Marxism
無政府主義	Nationalism
個人主義	Communism
	Internationalism

* * *

Here are a few of Ms. Li's comments, but some of the words are missing. See if you can fill in the blanks without listening to the monologue. Then check to see if you are right by playing the audio segment again.

教育	根本	不僅	為	對
期望	答對	不及格	帶	共享

1. 像念書一樣，這裡念書都是_____你自己，可是在臺灣你_____是_____自己念書。你念書的時候還_____著你家裡人_____你的_____。

2. 在中國的_____裡面，你十二個裡面只_____了六個，那個_____就是_____的。

Now go back and translate these sentences into English.

_____

_____

_____

_____

Follow-up Activities 應用

大家來讀 Role-Playing (Reading)

Here's Li Yinghui's ID card from Taiwan. Answer the following questions based on the information on this card.

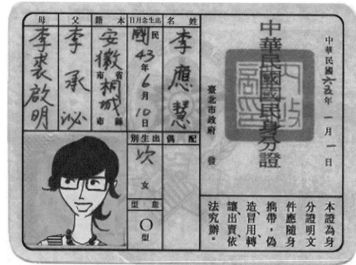

What are her parents' names?

_____

When was she born? (Do you remember how dates are indicated in Taiwan?)

_____

What is her blood type?

_____

When was this card issued?

_____

What is her 本籍 (běnjí: ancestral native place)?

_____

Here is a table comparing the number of days that students in various countries are required to attend school.

Country			Length of School Year in Days
中國			251
日本			243
韓國	Hánguó	Korea	220
以色列	Yǐsèliè	Israel	215
德國	Déguó	Germany	210
俄國	Éguó	Russia	210
瑞士	Ruìshì	Switzerland	207
荷蘭	Hélán	The Netherlands	200
蘇格蘭	Sūgélán	Scotland	200
泰國	Tàiguó	Thailand	200
美國			180

When Ms. Li saw this chart, she became even more concerned about the current problems in American education. With a partner, imagine that she is discussing this situation with one of her children's teachers.

大家來寫 Role-Playing (Written)

Write a short narrative in Chinese from the perspective of one of Ms. Li's children describing the incident she recounted involving Chinese vs. American table manners.

_____

_____

_____

_____

_____

_____

_____

_____

_____

_____

_____

_____

Preparation 熱身

Useful Vocabulary

熱潮	rècháo	N	upsurge
懷舊	huáijiù	V	to yearn for the past
傳統	chuántǒng	Adj, N	traditional, tradition
現象	xiànxiàng	N	phenomenon
志願軍	zhìyuànjūn	N	volunteer army
犧牲	xīshēng	V, N	to sacrifice, sacrifice
事蹟	shìjī	N	a person's lifetime accomplishments
抒情	shūqíng	Adj	lyrical
		V O	to express one's emotions
高昂	gāo'áng	Adj	exalted, elated
搖滾樂	yáogǔnyuè	N	rock 'n' roll
符合	fúhé	V	to accord with
反映	fǎnyìng	V	to reflect
懷疑	huáiyí	V, N	to suspect, to doubt; suspicion, doubt
分析	fēnxi, fēnxī	V, N	to analyze, analysis
咬字	yǎozì	V O	to "over-enunciate" lyrics, an operatic technique in which the singer exaggerates the lyrics

Additional Vocabulary

Match these words to the corresponding English meanings.

_____	樂器	a. solo
_____	歌詞	b. to give an instrumental performance
_____	炮聲	c. singing style
_____	樂隊	d. singer, vocalist
_____	歌手	e. to sing in performance
_____	演唱	f. musical instrument
_____	女高音	g. main theme
_____	主題	h. lyrics
_____	獨唱	i. sound of artillery
_____	唱法	j. orchestra, band
_____	演奏	k. soprano

In Communist China, politics became all-powerful. The Central Philharmonic Society, established in Beijing in 1956, was urged to play even more Chinese pieces… Mao Zedong had denounced art for art's sake. "All culture or literature and art belongs to a definite class and party, and has a definite political line."

— *New Asia Review*, charter issue (1994): 28.30

The so-called "revolutionary song" you are about to hear was actually a patriotic piece, in contrast to the internationalism in its French counterpart, *L'internationale*. This song was written to praise a soldier of the Liberation Army, who died on the battlefield, as a national hero.

Before listening to the audio segment, circle the characteristics that you think might be typical of a Chinese revolutionary song:

Tone	Tempo	Theme	Image	Main Instruments
sorrowful	very slow	internationalism	lovers	flute
satirical	slow	humanism	soldiers	piano
lyrical	quick	patriotism	intellectuals	harp
majestic	very quick		bourgeoisie	drum

▶ Listening for the Gist 泛聽

In this program the radio announcer did **not...**

	✓
give historical background for the songs.	
make a comparison between the songs.	
mention the name of the hero's sister.	
mention the singers' names.	

The relationship of the first song to the second is...

	✓
the same song sung in a different dialect.	
a traditional versus a modern adaptation.	
a different version sung by the same singer.	
the same music with different lyrics.	
There is no relation between the two songs.	

As you listen to these songs, identify which has these characteristics:

	Song #1	Song #2
50s/60s		
rock		
female singer		
clear pronunciation		
playful tone		
husky voice		
jazz		

▶ Listening for Details 靜聽

Match each of the topics on the left with the appropriate item on the right:

name of the movie	你唱我唱大家唱
hero of the story	英雄兒女
a historical event	抗美援潮戰爭
	王成

Based on this radio program, determine if the following statements are true (是) or false (非):

重唱革命歌曲是中國近幾年來的一股懷舊熱潮。	是	非
《英雄兒女》是七十年代的小說。	是	非
王成在戰爭中犧牲了，他的妹妹王芳也犧牲了。	是	非
歌手受過傳統的音樂訓練。	是	非
第二首歌反映了現代年輕人對共產主義懷疑的態度。	是	非
勇士腐爛變泥土，敵人輝煌化金星。	是	非

Key Language Points 語言點

Answer the following questions in Chinese based on what was said in this radio program, using the words or expressions in parentheses in your answer.

1. 革命曲跟中國七十年代的社會有什麼關係？(反映)

_____

2. 根據這位節目主持人，傳統的唱法跟現代的唱法有什麼不同？
   (保持)

_____

3. 第一首歌和第二首歌的歌詞跟音樂有差別嗎？(符合)

_____

4. 如果你不同意節目主持人這樣分析這兩首歌曲，你可以做什麼？
(同樣時間)

_____

＊　＊　＊

一向，甚至，總之

Do you remember hearing these expressions in the radio broadcast? If not, go back and listen again and see if you can figure out how they are used. Give a rough translation or paraphrase (in English) of the sentences in which these expressions occur.

一向

_____

_____

甚至

_____

_____

總之 (abbreviated form of 總而言之)

_____

Now fill in the blanks in the following sentences with the appropriate one of these expressions and then translate each sentence into English.

1. 現在住在大陸的中國人_____認為革命曲是當代中國歷史的一部分。

   _____

2. 很多年輕人覺得國歌對自己，對父母，_____對祖宗，都有相當大的的意義。

   _____

3. _____他們以這類的音樂為重要的研究項目。

   _____

Follow-up Activities 應用

大家來說 Role-Playing (Oral)

With a partner, imagine that one person is a disc jockey and the other is a listener who is calling in to request a song. Be sure to discuss your individual preferences in music, such as favorite performers, composers, and styles of music, and be prepared to defend or explain your choices.

大家來寫 **Role-Playing (Written)**

Fill in the lyrics based on what you heard in this program. A list of words from which you can choose is given below. Some words may be used more than once.

地　血　花　為　鮮　大　麼　開　什

_____ _____ _____戰旗美如畫？

英雄的 _____ _____染紅了它。

為什麼_____ _____春常在？

英雄的生命_____ _____ _____。

Now translate this stanza into English:

_____

_____

_____

_____

Vocabulary Index

生詞表

Pinyin	Traditional Characters	Simplified Characters	Lesson Number
bāojiǎozi	包餃子	包饺子	37
bāokuò	包括	包括	18
bǎochí	保持	保持	23
bǎoxiǎn	保險	保险	31
bǎozhòngshēntǐ	保重身體	保重身体	8
bào	抱	抱	38
běi	北	北	1
běnjí	本籍	本藉	44
bízi	鼻子	鼻子	38
bǐjiào (jiǎo)	比較	比较	12
bǐsài	比賽	比赛	33
bǐlì	筆力	笔力	35
bìyè	畢業	毕业	2
biānjí	編輯	编辑	17
biàndāng	便當	便当	32
biànhuà	變化	变化	22
biāozhì	標誌	标志	26
bīng	冰	冰	36
bōlí	玻璃	玻璃	31
bózi	脖子	脖子	30
bóshì (xuéwèi)	博士（學位）	博士（学位）	34, 40
búguò	不過	不过	25
bú (yòng) kèqì	不（用）客氣	不（用）客气	3
bú (yòng) xiè	不（用）謝	不（用）谢	3
bùduōjiǔ	不多久	不多久	14
bùjígé	不及格	不及格	44

Pinyin	Traditional Characters	Simplified Characters	Lesson Number
(bù) jǐnjǐn	（不）僅僅	（不）仅仅	44
bùzěnmezàiháng	不怎麼在行	不怎么在行	37
bùxíng	步行	步行	26
bùzhòu	步驟	步骤	35

C

cáiliào	材料	材料	14
càipǔ	菜譜	菜谱	37
cánjí	殘疾	残疾	42
cǎn	慘	惨	39
cǎonǐ	草擬	草拟	42
cè	測	测	26
chá	查	查	13
cházìdiǎn	查字典	查字典	13
chá	茶	茶	5
cháchǐ	茶匙	茶匙	37
chà (chā)	差	差	33
chà(chā)bùduō	差不多	差不多	30
chāyì	差異	差异	42
chà(chā)yìdiǎn(r)	差一點兒	差一点儿	30
chāi fángzi	拆房子	拆房子	22
cháng(yicháng)	嚐（一嚐）	尝（一尝）	29
chángshòu	長壽	长寿	15
chàngfǎ	唱法	唱法	45
chāozhòng	超重	超重	23
cháoshī	潮濕	潮湿	10

Pinyin	Traditional Characters	Simplified Characters	Lesson Number
chǎojià	吵架	吵架	39
chēwèi	車位	车位	18
chèdǐ	徹底	彻底	33
chènshān	襯衫	衬衫	9
chīsù	吃素	吃素	12
chídào	遲到	迟到	10
chōngjī	衝擊	冲击	43
chōngjì	沖劑	冲剂	30
chōng	衝	冲	31
chōngtū	衝突	冲突	39
chōuyān	抽煙	抽烟	23
chūfā	出發	出发	27
chūzūqìchē	出租汽車	出租汽车	11
chūqī	初期	初期	30
chuán	船	船	11
chuánshòu	傳授	传授	43
chuántǒng	傳統	传统	45
chuánzhēnjī	傳真機	传真机	23
chuàngzào	創造	创造	29
chuàngzàolì	創造力	创造力	35
chūnjià	春假	春假	11
chūnjié	春節	春节	12
chūntiān	春天	春天	10
cí	詞	词	40
cōng	蔥	葱	37
cóngláibù/méi	從來不/沒	从来不/没	10

Pinyin	Traditional Characters	Simplified Characters	Lesson Number
D			
dādàng	搭檔	搭档	33
dáduì	答對	答对	44
dǎ bàngqiú	打棒球	打棒球	20
dǎ lánqiú	打籃球	打篮球	20
dǎ pīngpāngqiú	打乒乓球	打乒乓球	20
dǎrǎo	打擾	打扰	28
dǎsàn	打散	打散	29
dǎsuàn	打算	打算	21
dǎ wǎngqiú	打網球	打网球	20
dǎzhé	打折	打折	21
dǎzhēn	打針	打针	16
dàbáicài	大白菜	大白菜	37
dàduōshù	大多數	大多数	30
dàgài	大概	大概	9
dāgēdà	大哥大	大哥大	41
dài(yī)huǐ(r)	待（一）會兒	待（一）会儿	5
dàifū	大夫	大夫	30
dàijià	代價	代价	38
dài	帶	带	28, 44
dàizi	帶子	带子	9
dài	袋	袋	30
dāndú	單獨	单独	17
dānwèi	單位	单位	17
dàngāo	蛋糕	蛋糕	15
dāng	當	当	2

Pinyin	Traditional Characters	Simplified Characters	Lesson Number
dàochù	到處	到处	22
dào...wéizhǐ	到⋯為止	到⋯为止	40
dào	倒	倒	16
dàobié	道別	道别	23
dé	得	得	16
dēng	燈	灯	36
dēnglóng	燈籠	灯笼	25
děng yí xià	等一下	等一下	5
děng yì huǐ(r)	等一會兒	等一会儿	5
dìdào	地道	地道	32
dìdiǎn	地點	地点	18
dì(lǐ)xué	地（理）學	地（理）学	1
diǎnxíng	典型	典型	35
diànchē	電車	电车	11
diànnǎo	電腦	电脑	13
diàntī	電梯	电梯	32
diànyǐngyuàn	電影院	电影院	14
diànzǐyóujiàn	電子郵件	电子邮件	23
diāo	雕	雕	36
diào	掉	掉	21
diàochá	調查	调查	42
diē	爹	爹	38
dìng	訂	订	15
dōng	東	东	1
dōngtiān	冬天	冬天	10
dòngwùyuán	動物園	动物园	26

Pinyin	Traditional Characters	Simplified Characters	Lesson Number
dòufu	豆腐	豆腐	37
dòu(fǔ)gān	豆（腐）乾	豆（腐）乾	37
dú	讀	读	13
dúzhě	讀者	读者	33
dúchàng	獨唱	独唱	45
duǎn	短	短	13
duǎnzhàn	短暫	短暂	11
duì	對	对	26, 44
duìbùqǐ	對不起	对不起	27
duìmiàn	對面	对面	1
dùn	燉	炖	29
duōyīnzì	多音字	多音字	17
duōyú	多餘	多余	44
duōyún	多雲	多云	10

E

Pinyin	Traditional Characters	Simplified Characters	Lesson Number
érqiě	而且	而且	21
ěrduo	耳朵	耳朵	38

F

Pinyin	Traditional Characters	Simplified Characters	Lesson Number
fāshāo	發燒	发烧	16
fānqié	番茄	番茄	24
fǎn	反	反	27
fǎnyìng	反映	反映	45
fǎnzhèng	反正	反正	16
fàncuòwù	犯錯誤	犯错误	37
fànhé	飯盒	饭盒	32

Pinyin	Traditional Characters	Simplified Characters	Lesson Number
fāngfǎ	方法	方法	11
fāngshì	方式	方式	40
fángdōng	房東	房东	18
fángzū	房租	房租	18
fàngsōng	放鬆	放松	33
fēicháng	非常	非常	2
fēijī	飛機	飞机	11
fēnxī	分析	分析	45
fèndòu	奮鬥	奋斗	41
fēngwèi	風味	风味	12
fūfù	夫婦	夫妇	17
fú	扶	扶	38
fúhé	符合	符合	45
fúwù	服務	服务	27
fúzhuāng	服裝	服装	9
fù	賦	赋	40
fùzá	複雜	复杂	20
fùzhàng	付帳	付帐	14

G

gǎi	改	改	8
gài fángzi	蓋房子	盖房子	22
gàizhāng	蓋章	盖章	44
gān	乾	乾	29
gānjìng	乾淨	乾净	22
gānzào	乾燥	乾燥	10

Pinyin	Traditional Characters	Simplified Characters	Lesson Number
gǎn	趕	赶	30
gǎnjué	感覺	感觉	7
gǎnmào	感冒	感冒	16
gǎnxiè	感謝	感谢	3
gǎnlǎnqiú	橄欖球	橄榄球	20
gǎnpí	擀皮	擀皮	37
gǎnshòu	感受	感受	35
gāo'áng	高昂	高昂	45
gāolóu	高樓	高楼	22
gāosùgōnglù	高速公路	高速公路	11
gǎo	搞	搞	27
gē	擱	搁	29
gēcí	歌詞	歌词	45
gēshǒu	歌手	歌手	45
gè	各	各	36
gè	個	个	36
gèdì	各地	各地	36
gèrénzhǔyì	個人主義	个人主义	44
gēnběn	根本	根本	7, 36, 44
gēnyuán	根源	根源	39
gōnggòngqìchē	公共汽車	公共汽车	11
gōnglù	公路	公路	11
gōnglì	功力	功力	35
gòngchǎnzhǔyì	共產主義	共产主义	44
gòngxiǎng	共享	共享	44
gòuwù zhōngxīn	購物中心	购物中心	14

Pinyin	Traditional Characters	Simplified Characters	Lesson Number
gūdān	孤單	孤单	41
gǔdiǎn wénxué	古典文學	古典文学	40
gǔlì	鼓勵	鼓励	44
guāfēng	刮風	刮风	10
guà	掛	挂	25
guàibudé	怪不得	怪不得	2
guāndiǎn	觀點	观点	40
guàn	罐	罐	24
guànshū	灌輸	灌输	43
guànxǐshì	盥洗室	盥洗室	28
guāngmíng	光明	光明	39
guīzé	規則	规则	33
guójì	國際	国际	19
guójìzhǔyì	國際主義	国际主义	44
guójiā	國家	国家	12
guǒzhī	果汁	果汁	5

H

Pinyin	Traditional Characters	Simplified Characters	Lesson Number
hǎixiā	海蝦	海虾	24
hánjià	寒假	寒假	11
háofù	豪富	豪富	41
hǎobùliǎo	好不了	好不了	16
hǎojǐtiān	好幾天	好几天	16
héshì	合適	合适	18
héfàn	盒飯	盒饭	32
hézi	盒子	盒子	19

Pinyin	Traditional Characters	Simplified Characters	Lesson Number
hèn	恨	恨	22
hōngdòng	轟動	轰动	41
hónglǜdēng	紅綠燈	红绿灯	14
hǒng	哄	哄	38
hòu	後	后	1
hòulái	後來	后来	4
hú	湖	湖	1
huáqiáo	華僑	华侨	8
huáyì	華裔	华裔	8
huáxuě	滑雪	滑雪	20
huàxué	化學	化学	1
huáijiù	懷舊	怀旧	45
huáiyí	懷疑	怀疑	45
huānlè	歡樂	欢乐	41
huānyíng guānglín	歡迎光臨	欢迎光临	14
huàn	換	换	18
huànqián	換錢	换钱	23
huāng	慌	慌	31
huí	回	回	27
huódòng	活動	活动	4
huópō	活潑	活泼	35
huóyuè	活躍	活跃	35
huǒchē	火車	火车	11
huómiàn	和麵	和面	37
hùzhào	護照	护照	23

Pinyin	Traditional Characters	Simplified Characters	Lesson Number
J			
jīdàn	雞蛋	鸡蛋	24
jītuǐ	雞腿	鸡腿	24
jīhū	幾乎	几乎	30
jīliè	激烈	激烈	42
jīpiào	機票	机票	23
jígé	及格	及格	44
jíhé	集合	集合	32
jì	寄	寄	19
jìcúnchù	寄存處	寄存处	32
jì	繫	系	31
jìchéngchē	計程車	计程车	11
jìnéng	技能	技能	42
jìniànpǐn	紀念品	纪念品	32
jìzhě	記者	记者	33
jìyìlì	記憶力	记忆力	35
jiāchángcài	家常菜	家常菜	29
jiānchí	堅持	坚持	40
jiǎn	剪	剪	27
jiǎnchá	檢查	检查	23
jiànkāng	健康	健康	16
jiànyì	建議	建议	36
jiànzhù	建築	建筑	42
jiāng	薑	姜	37
jiǎngjiù	講究	讲究	15

Pinyin	Traditional Characters	Simplified Characters	Lesson Number
jiāohuàn	交換	交换	40
jiāoliú	交流	交流	40
jiāotōng	交通	交通	18
jiāoshū	教書	教书	8
jiǎodù	角度	角度	40
jiǎotàchē	腳踏車	脚踏车	11
jiǎozi	餃子	饺子	37
jiǎozipí	餃子皮	饺子皮	37
jiàoshì	教室	教室	1
jiàoyù	教育	教育	44
jiàoyùchéngdù	教育程度	教育程度	27
jiē	接	接	11
jiēshí	結實	结实	34
jiēzhe+verb	接著+verb	接著+verb	36
jiémùzhǔchǐrén	節目主持人	节目主持人	42
jīn	斤	斤	24
jǐn	緊	紧	37
jìnbù	進步	进步	7
jīngcháng	經常	经常	14
jīnglìchōngfèn	精力充分	精力充分	33
jīngxǐ	驚喜	惊喜	35
jiǔcài	韭菜	韭菜	37
jiùshìshuō	就是說	就是说	2
júhuā	菊花	菊花	24, 29
jùtǐ	具體	具体	39
juéduìbù/méi	絕對不/沒	绝对不/没	9

Pinyin	Traditional Characters	Simplified Characters	Lesson Number
K			
kāfēi	咖啡	咖啡	5
kāishuǐ	開水	开水	5
kāixīn	開心	开心	16
kànbàozhǐ	看報紙	看报纸	7
kàndiànshì	看電視	看电视	7
kànzhàopiàn	看照片	看照片	7
(kǎoshì) juànzi	（考試）卷子	（考试）卷子	43
kēzé	苛責	苛责	44
késòu	咳嗽	咳嗽	16
kě	可	可	40
kěguānde shùmù	可觀的數目	可观的数目	40
kělè	可樂	可乐	5
kèchéng	課程	课程	34
kètīng	客廳	客厅	18
kěndìng	肯定	肯定	9
kōngqìwūrǎn	空氣污染	空气污染	23
kōngxū	空虛	空虚	41
kǒngjù	恐懼	恐惧	41
kǒngpà	恐怕	恐怕	11
kǔ	苦	苦	12
kùzi	褲子	裤子	9
kuàizi	筷子	筷子	24
kùn	睏	困	38

Pinyin	Traditional Characters	Simplified Characters	Lesson Number
L			
là	辣	辣	12
láojià	勞駕	劳驾	28
lǎobǎn	老闆	老板	14
lǎorén	老人	老人	15
lǎorénjiā	老人家	老人家	32
lèyú	樂於	乐于	35
lèi	累	累	6
lèi	類	类	27
lèisì	類似	类似	35
lěng	冷	冷	10
lěngdàn	冷淡	冷淡	41
lěngqì	冷氣	冷气	16
lǐfà(fǎ)diàn	理髮店	理发店	27
lǐlùn	理論	理沦	40
lǐjiě	理解	理解	2
lǐwù	禮物	礼物	15
lián...dōu/yě	連…都/也	连…都/也	18
liánluò	聯絡	联络	23
liánxì	聯繫	联系	23
liàn jiànshù	練劍術	练剑术	20
liàn tàijíquán	練太極拳	练太极拳	20
liángkuài	涼快	凉快	10
liàngcí	量詞	量词	17
liáotiān(r)	聊天（兒）	聊天（儿）	5
liǎobùqǐ	了不起	了不起	34

Pinyin	Traditional Characters	Simplified Characters	Lesson Number
lǐngdài	領帶	领带	9
liūbīng	溜冰	溜冰	20
liú	留	留	17
liúxuéshēng	留學生	留学生	12
liúxíng	流行	流行	5
liúxuè	流血	流血	31
lóng	龍	龙	15
lóu	樓	楼	1
lùxù	陸續	陆续	43
lùlùxùxùde	陸陸續續地	陆陆续续地	43
lǚxíngtuán	旅行團	旅行团	32
lǚyóu	旅遊	旅游	21
luàn	亂	乱	13
lúnyǐ	輪椅	轮椅	42
lùnwén	論文	论文	30, 40

M

máfán	麻煩	麻烦	11, 28
mǎkèsīzhǔyì	馬克思主義	马克思主义	44
mǎlù	馬路	马路	14
màibó	脈搏	脉搏	30
mǎntóudàhàn	滿頭大汗	满头大汗	20
máodùn	矛盾	矛盾	41
máoyī	毛衣	毛衣	9
màozi	帽子	帽子	9
méiguīhuā	玫瑰花	玫瑰花	24

Pinyin	Traditional Characters	Simplified Characters	Lesson Number
méimáo	眉毛	眉毛	38
méiguānxi	沒關係	没关系	27
méishì(r)	沒事儿	没事儿	13
méishénme	沒有什麼	没有什麼	3
měi...dōu...	每⋯都⋯	每⋯都⋯	12
Měiguórén	美國人	美国人	4
měishì zúqiú	美式足球	美式足球	20
mēn	悶	闷	10
ménkǒu	門口	门口	25
mí	迷	迷	26
mílù	迷路	迷路	26
mǐ	米	米	26
miàn	麵	面	15
miàntiáo	麵條	面条	15
miào	妙	妙	41
mínzúzhǔyì	民族主義	民族主义	44
mǐn'gǎn	敏感	敏感	39
míngxìnpiàn	明信片	明信片	19
mógu (dōnggu)	蘑菇（冬菇）	蘑菇（冬菇）	37
mótuōchē	摩托車	摩托车	11
mòshēng	陌生	陌生	41
mǔyǔ	母語	母语	2

N

náshǒucài	拿手菜	拿手菜	29
nǎlǐnǎlǐ	哪裏哪裏	哪里哪里	3

Pinyin	Traditional Characters	Simplified Characters	Lesson Number
nàjiùsuànle	那就算了	那就算了	28
nà yě kěyǐ	那也可以	那也可以	3
nán	南	南	1
nánzhuāng	男裝	男装	9
nǎodài téng	腦袋疼	脑袋疼	30
nǐ gànmá ne	你幹嘛呢	你干嘛呢	13
niàobù	尿布	尿布	38
niúnǎi	牛奶	牛奶	5, 24
niúròu	牛肉	牛肉	24
nóngmín	農民	农民	24
nǚgāoyīn	女高音	女高音	45
nǚquánzhǔyì	女權主義	女权主义	44
nǚzhuāng	女裝	女装	9

P

pāi zhàopiàn	拍照片	拍照片	7
páiduì	排隊	排队	27
páijià	牌價	牌价	24
pángbiān	旁邊	旁边	1
pǎobù	跑步	跑步	20
pàochá	泡茶	泡茶	29
pào(kāi)	泡（開）	泡（开）	29
pàoshēng	炮聲	炮声	45
péi	陪	陪	27
píjiǔ	啤酒	啤酒	5, 24
píláo	疲勞	疲劳	30

Pinyin	Traditional Characters	Simplified Characters	Lesson Number
pínglùn	評論	评论	39
pínglùnjiā	評論家	评论家	39
pòpòlànlàn	破破爛爛	破破烂烂	41
pòyīnzì	破音字	破音字	17
pūchuáng	鋪床	铺床	44
pǔtōng	普通	普通	29
Q			
qīwàng	期望	期望	44
qíshí	其實	其实	16
qìchē	汽車	汽车	11
qìshuǐ	汽水	汽水	5, 24
qìhòu	氣候	气候	22
qiàqià	恰恰	恰恰	35
qiānwàn búyào/bié	千萬不要/別	千万不要/别	29
qiānxū	謙虛	谦虚	33
qiānzhèng	簽證	签证	18, 23
qián	前	前	1
qiánhòu	前後	前後	30
qiáng	牆	墙	14
qiǎo	巧	巧	34
qīngdàn	清淡	清淡	12
qīngsōng	輕鬆	轻松	4
qīngxǐng	清醒	清醒	33
qíng	晴	晴	10
qíngkuàng	情況	情况	13

Pinyin	Traditional Characters	Simplified Characters	Lesson Number
qìngzhù	慶祝	庆祝	17
qiūtiān	秋天	秋天	10
qū	區	区	34
qǔjīng	取經	取经	37
qǔshě	取捨	取舍	43
qùdiào	去掉	去掉	37
quán	全	全	2
quánlì	權力	权力	35
quàn	勸	劝	16
quēxiàn	缺陷	缺陷	42
qúnzi	裙子	裙子	9

R

Pinyin	Traditional Characters	Simplified Characters	Lesson Number
rè	熱	热	10
rècháo	熱潮	热潮	45
rènào	熱鬧	热闹	36
rónghé	融合	融合	44
róngxìng	榮幸	荣幸	39
rúcǐ	如此	如此	34
rúguǒ...dehuà	如果…的話	如果…的话	11
rúhé	如何	如何	43

S

Pinyin	Traditional Characters	Simplified Characters	Lesson Number
sāichē	塞車	塞车	22
shǎn (kāi)	閃（開）	闪（开）	31
shāngchǎng	商場	商场	15

Pinyin	Traditional Characters	Simplified Characters	Lesson Number
shāngliang	商量	商量	28
shàng	上	上	1
shàngxià	上下	上下	30
shàngxué	上學	上学	8
shāowēi	稍微	稍微	24
shétou	舌頭	舌头	30
shèhuìzhǔyì	社會主義	社会主义	44
shèshī	設施	设施	32, 42
shēn	伸	伸	30
shēngāo	身高	身高	38
shēntǐ	身體	身体	2
shénmede	什麼的	什么的	7
shènzhì	甚至	甚至	45
shēngcài	生菜	生菜	24
shēngchéng	生成	生成	43
shēnghuó	生活	生活	5
shēngwù (xué)	生物（學）	生物（学）	1
shěng	省	省	19
shī	詩	诗	40
shīfu	師傅	师傅	12
shīqùzhījué	失去知覺	失去知觉	31
shīzi	獅子	狮子	26
shíjìshàng	實際上	实际上	13
shítou	石頭	石头	26
shízìlùkǒu	十字路口	十字路口	14

Pinyin	Traditional Characters	Simplified Characters	Lesson Number
shìjī	事蹟	事迹	45
shìyàn	試驗	试验	35
shōu	收	收	19
shōudào	收到	收到	2
shōujù	收據	收据	14
shǒutào	手套	手套	20
shǒuxiān	首先	首先	29
shòu	瘦	瘦	16
shòushāng	受傷	受伤	31
shūfú	舒服	舒服	10
shūjià	書架	书架	13
shūmíng	書名	书名	13
shūqíng	抒情	抒情	45
shú(shóu)xi	熟悉	熟悉	12
shǔjià	暑假	暑假	11
shù	束	束	24
shuǐ	水	水	5
shuǐdiànfèi	水電費	水电费	18
shuìmián	睡眠	睡眠	30
shuōfúlì	說服力	说服力	35
shuōláijiùcháng	說來就長	说来就长	17
shuòshì (xuéwèi)	碩士（學位）	硕士（学位）	34, 40
sījī	司機	司机	31
sīwéi	思維	思维	35
sòng	送	送	11
suān	酸	酸	12

Pinyin	Traditional Characters	Simplified Characters	Lesson Number
suì	碎	碎	31
suǒyǐ shuō	所以說	所以说	37
T			
tàidù	態度	态度	40
tāngchí	湯匙	汤匙	37
tǎng	躺	躺	16
tǎorén xǐhuān	討人喜歡	讨人喜欢	38
tèbié	特別	特别	16
tèjià	特價	特价	5
tīzúqiú	踢足球	踢足球	20
tíqián	提前	提前	11
tíxǐng	提醒	提醒	16
tǐyùguǎn	體育館	体育馆	1
tǐwēn	體溫	体温	30
tǐzhòng	體重	体重	38
tián	甜	甜	12
tián	填	填	27
tiánbiǎo	填表	填表	27
tiāo	挑	挑	9
tiáoxiàn	調餡	调馅	37
tiē	貼	贴	19
tīng guǎngbō	聽廣播	听广播	7
tǐnghǎo	挺好	挺好	3
tōng	通	通	34
tōngdào	通道	通道	42

Pinyin	Traditional Characters	Simplified Characters	Lesson Number
tóngyàng	同樣	同样	44
tóufa	頭髮	头发	17, 27
tóuténg	頭疼	头疼	30
tūrán	突然	突然	31, 32
tǔshēng tǔzhǎng	土生土長	土生土长	44
tuìxiū	退休	退休	2
tuō	拖	拖	16
tuōěrsuǒ	托兒所	托儿所	43

W

wàzi	襪子	袜子	9
wàitào	外套	外套	9
wán(r)	玩（兒）	玩（儿）	4
wēixiǎn	危險	危险	11
wèi	餵	喂	38
wèi	為	为	44
wèidào	味道	味道	12
wèikǒu	胃口	胃口	30
wèimíng	未名	未名	1
wénjiàn	文件	文件	23
wénshǐ	文史	文史	1
wényánwén	文言文	文言文	40
wòshì	臥室	卧室	18
wūrǎn	污染	污染	22
wúfǎ	無法	无法	35
wúzhèngfǔzhǔyì	無政府主義	无政府主义	44

Pinyin	Traditional Characters	Simplified Characters	Lesson Number
X			
xī	西	西	1
xīhóngshì	西紅柿	西红柿	24
xīzhuāng	西裝	西装	9
xīshēng	犧牲	牺牲	45
xíguàn	習慣	习惯	5
xǐzǎojiān	洗澡間	洗澡间	18
xì	系	系	1
xià	下	下	1
xiàxuě	下雪	下雪	10
xiàyǔ	下雨	下雨	10
xiàtiān	夏天	夏天	10
xián	鹹	咸	12, 29
xiàn	限	限	27
xiànzhì	限制	限制	42
xiànchéng	現成	现成	37
xiànjīn	現金	现金	14
xiànxiàng	現象	现象	45
xiàndài wénxué	現代文學	现代文学	40
xiàn(jìnqù)	陷（進去）	陷（进去）	31
xiāngdāng (yú)	相當（於）	相当（于）	42
xiāngfǎn	相反	相反	35
xiǎngxiàng	想像	想像	22
xiàng..guǎi	向…拐	向…拐	14
xiàng(...děngděng)	像（…等等）	象（…等等）	12

Pinyin	Traditional Characters	Simplified Characters	Lesson Number
xiǎochī	小吃	小吃	36
xiǎodāo	小刀	小刀	14
xiǎopéngyǒu	小朋友	小朋友	15
xiǎoshí	小時	小时	25
xiàolǜ	效率	效率	33
xiàoyuán	校園	校园	14
xiélì	協力	协力	35
xiézi	鞋子	鞋子	9
xīnxiān	新鮮	新鲜	29
xìnfēng	信封	信封	19
xínglǐ	行李	行李	11
xíngwéi	行為	行为	39
xìng	性	性	33
xìngbié	性別	性别	27
xìngkuī	幸虧	幸亏	31
xìngqù	興趣	兴趣	7
xiōngdì jiěmèi	兄弟姐妹	兄弟姐妹	2
xūzì	虛字	虚字	40
xuǎn	選	选	8
xuéwèi	學位	学位	34
xuézhě	學者	学者	33
xuètǒng	血統	血统	43
xúnzhǎo	尋找	寻找	39
xùnliàn	訓練	训练	33

Pinyin	Traditional Characters	Simplified Characters	Lesson Number
Y			
yājīn	押金	押金	18
yán	沿	沿	26
yángé	嚴格	严格	43
yánjǐn	嚴謹	严谨	35
yánzhòng	嚴重	严重	16
yǎnchàng	演唱	演唱	45
yǎnzòu	演奏	演奏	45
yǎnjīng	眼睛	眼睛	38
yǎnlèi	眼淚	眼泪	20
yāo	幺	幺	31
yáogǔnyuè	搖滾樂	摇滚乐	45
yáoyuǎn	遙遠	遥远	41
yǎozì	咬字	咬字	45
yào	藥	药	16
yàobù (rán)	要不（然）	要不（然）	12
yàoshì..dehuà	要是…的話	要是…的话	11
yěxǔ	也許	也许	9
yīshēng	醫生	医生	2
yīyuàn	醫院	医院	16
yímín	移民	移民	41
yíxiàng	一向	一向	45
yíxiàzi	一下子	一下子	16
yídìng	一定	一定	9
yítào	一套	一套	30
yǐshàng/xià	以上/下	以上/下	27

Pinyin	Traditional Characters	Simplified Characters	Lesson Number
yǐ…wéiróng	以···為榮	以···为荣	43
yìbān	一般	一般	30
yìhuǐ(r)	一會兒	一会儿	16
yìwài	意外	意外	39
yìxìng	異性	异性	39
yīn	陰	阴	10
yǐnqǐ	引起	引起	39
yìnxiàng	印象	印象	34
yìnxiàngzhǔyì	印象主義	印象主义	44
yīng'ér	嬰兒	婴儿	32
yòng	用	用	14
yóu	油	油	12
yóu	郵	邮	19
yóujiàn	郵件	邮件	19
yóupiào	郵票	邮票	19
yóulǎn	遊覽	游览	32
yóuqí(shì)	尤其（是）	尤其（是）	40
yóuyǒng	游泳	游泳	20
yǒuxiào	有效	有效	30
yǒuxiàoguǒ	有效果	有效果	30
yòu'ér suǒ	幼兒所	幼儿所	43
yòu'ér yuán	幼兒園	幼儿园	43
yòuzhì yuán	幼稚園	幼稚园	43
yú	魚	鱼	24
yǔmáoqiú	羽毛球	羽毛球	33
yǔsǎn	雨傘	雨伞	9

Pinyin	Traditional Characters	Simplified Characters	Lesson Number
yùgāng	浴缸	浴缸	28
yùliào	預料	预料	39
yuánlái	原來	原来	4
yuánzhuō	圓桌	圆桌	44
yuànyì	願意	愿意	12
yuèláiyuè	越來越	越来越	7
yuèduì	樂隊	乐队	45
yuèqì	樂器	乐器	45
yǔnxǔ	允許	允许	39
yùn	運	运	19

Z

Pinyin	Traditional Characters	Simplified Characters	Lesson Number
zánmen	咱們	咱们	1
zāng	髒	脏	22
zěnmebàn	怎麼辦	怎麼办	13
zěnmegǎode	怎麼搞的	怎麼搞的	27
zěnme huí shì(r)	怎麼回事兒	怎麼回事儿	27
zhǎngwò	掌握	掌握	40
zhàng'ài	障礙	障碍	42
zhàngfū	丈夫	丈夫	17
zhāojí	著急	著急	7
zhāopái	招牌	招牌	14
zhàoxiàng	照相	照相	7
zhàoxiàngjī	照相機	照相机	7
zhéxué	哲學	哲学	1
zhě	者	者	33

Pinyin	Traditional Characters	Simplified Characters	Lesson Number
zhème...hái...	這麼⋯還⋯	这麼⋯还⋯	20
zhèyàng	這樣	这样	42
zhèyàngba	這樣吧	这样吧	28
zhēn búcuò	眞不錯	真不错	27
zhēnzhèng	眞正	真正	2
zhèng	正	正	26
zhèngcháng	正常	正常	30
zhènghǎo	正好	正好	1
zhèngqián	掙錢	挣钱	41
zhī	枝	枝	24
zhī	隻	只	24
zhīhòu	之後	之后	14
zhīhūzhěyě	之乎者也	之乎者也	40
zhīpiào	支票	支票	27
zhīyīn	知音	知音	35
zhíyè	職業	职业	27
zhǐjiào	指教	指教	30
zhìbùliǎo	治不了	治不了	16
zhìshǎo	至少	至少	19
zhìyuànjūn	志願軍	志愿军	45
zhǒng	種	种	12
zhònglì	重力	重力	35
zhōunián	週年	周年	17
zhǔtí	主題	主题	45
zhǔyào	主要	主要	2
zhǔyì	主義	主义	44

Pinyin	Traditional Characters	Simplified Characters	Lesson Number
zhùyuàn	住院	住院	16
zhuān	專	专	42
zhuānyè	專業	专业	7, 33
zhuànqián	賺錢	赚钱	41
zhuāng	裝	装	19
zhuàng	撞	撞	31
zīběnzhǔyì	資本主義	资本主义	44
zìcóng	自從	自从	38
zìdòng	自動	自动	32
zìxìnxīn	自信心	自信心	44
zìxíngchē	自行車	自行车	11
zìzūnxīn	自尊心	自尊心	44
zōnghé	綜合	综合	43
zǒng(éryán)zhī	總（而言）之	总（而言）之	45
zǒu guòlái/qù	走過來/去	走过来/去	10
zūyuē qīxiàn	租約期限	租约期限	18
zuǐba	嘴巴	嘴巴	38
zuǒyòu	左右	左右	17, 30
zuòfǎ	做法	做法	29
zuòzhě	作者	作者	33